Em —

Shared good times?

All the rest.

24-3-15

Praise for *Making Things Happen*

"This is the story of a gifted man – blessed with good health and a discerning eye – more interested in what's right than who's right and, in his words, 'putting bread before circuses', believing, as I do, that a market economy needs a moral framework of trust and fairness. His co-founding of the Centre for Policy Studies did more than anything to change the course of post-war British politics, as it led a political revolution. Armed with 'there is an alternative', Mrs T. and Sir Keith Joseph boarded the Tory ship of state, threw the Heath crew overboard and sailed off in a different direction, breaking the post-war consensus. It has been my pleasure to work with him over the years. Discussing a huge variety of shared interests – which this book reveals – has been greatly rewarding, as I hope it will be to others."

– Frank Field, *Labour MP and former Cabinet minister*

"Nigel Vinson was an influential Thatcherite whose role in helping to reverse the direction of British politics has not, until now, been properly recognised. More remarkably, he exemplified – and continues to exemplify in his ninth decade – the so-called vigorous virtues that lay at the heart of the Thatcher programme. Entrepreneurial, dynamic, inventive, practical, patriotic, robust and optimistic, Vinson possesses in abundance those aspects of the national character that, for a time, were stifled by state control, but which Thatcher knew must be encouraged if Britain was to overcome its economic and political malaise."

– John O'Sullivan, *writer and former senior adviser to Margaret Thatcher*

"Nigel Vinson has a mind like a rapier, searching out the potential of new ideas and evaluates them. I would have loved to have had him as one of my PhD students."

– Professor Ian Fells, *academic and government adviser on energy strategy*

MAKING THINGS HAPPEN

MAKING THINGS HAPPEN

THE LIFE AND ORIGINAL THINKING OF
NIGEL VINSON

LORD VINSON OF RODDAM DENE
LVO DL FRSA FBIM

GERALD FROST

Biteback Publishing

First published in Great Britain in 2015 by
Biteback Publishing Ltd
Westminster Tower
3 Albert Embankment
London SE1 7SP
Copyright © Gerald Frost 2015

Gerald Frost has asserted his right under the Copyright, Designs and
Patents Act 1988 to be identified as the author of this work.

ISBN 978-1-84954-859-5

10 9 8 7 6 5 4 3 2 1

A CIP catalogue record for this book is available from the British Library.

Set in ITC New Baskerville Std

Printed and bound in Great Britain by
CPI Group (UK) Ltd, Croydon CR0 4YY

For Vonnie

Contents

Acknowledgements

Acknowledgements

THANKS ARE OWED to the many friends, colleagues and business and professional associates of Lord Vinson who collaborated in the writing of this book. I am also grateful to his three daughters, Bettina, Rowena and Nonie, for sharing their recollections of him with me.

In particular, I would like to record the help given by Michael Stoddart, John Whitmore, Linda Whetstone, the late Alan Collett, Gillian Coppins, Peter Blencowe, Peter Bedford, Sir Nigel Sherlock, Mark Cannon Brookes, Christian and Diana Schumacher, Lady Dione Digby, Tony

Glenton, Jenny Nicholson, John Theobald, Alan Milligan, Christopher Ward, the late Jeremy Peter-Hoblyn, Margaret Clark, Michael Galsworthy, Lady Mary Holborow, Janet Laycock, Revd Canon Robert Burston, Mike Fisher, Simon Webley, Viscount Ridley, Tim Hobson, Frank Field MP, and the late John Blundell. Thanks are also due to Nicola Gibb for her patient and invaluable assistance in preparing the text for publication.

A great debt of gratitude is owed to Lady Yvonne (Vonnie) Vinson, not only for her thoughtful suggestions and insights, but also for her generous hospitality during the several highly enjoyable visits I made to the Vinsons' Northumberland home to examine family papers.

Finally, I should like to thank my wife Meg for her constant encouragement and support.

Introduction

B
Y THE TIME he was thirty-nine, Nigel Vinson had achieved what many strive to achieve by the time they are sixty. He had created and built up a successful company and made enough money to retire, although it is unlikely that so active a man was ever tempted to do so. Despite not possessing a single technical qualification he had also established a reputation as an original thinker of ideas as well as new products, which is why he continues to be described in his passport as 'inventor'.

Plastic Coatings, the company he founded in 1952, was

one of the first to find the technical means to apply a coating of plastic to metal and to recognise the huge number of uses that this would have. Over the next fourteen years his workforce increased by some 20 per cent a year; by the time the company was successfully floated on the London Stock Exchange in 1969 it was the largest of its kind in Europe, employing over 1,000 people in five different UK locations. Vinson had always disliked large-scale production units and hated the then fashionable belief that big was beautiful.

The company, which he had started in a single Nissen hut in Guildford seventeen years earlier with one employee and a secretary, was now a substantial concern and set to grow still larger.

In the past, Vinson had welcomed every new employee with a handshake, if possible on his or her first day. Developing employment policies, which were far advanced for their time and subsequently copied by others (and now would be called Quaker Capitalism), he had systematically eliminated the distinction between 'workers' and 'staff'. But the company had grown to the point where it was no longer possible to maintain the same level of personal involvement. When, to use one of Vinson's favourite phrases, it was no longer possible 'to walk the ship', he realised that life was not going to be as rewarding as in the past.

At the company's flotation, he remarkably gave 10 per cent of the proceeds to the workforce in the form of share options in recognition of their contribution to the company's success. Two years later, while still owning 54 per cent of what was then a public company, he agreed to sell his majority holding to Imperial Tobacco who were looking to diversify, continuing as chairman until they were satisfied that the business had settled down under its new management. No contract was deemed necessary – a handshake was sufficient to seal the arrangement. Vinson, a non-smoker, turned down a place on the Imperial Board. Having ceased to walk the ship, he walked away, explaining to friends that he saw no point in spending the rest of his life amassing wealth for its own sake.

Vinson's subsequent career, which has been no less remarkable, reflected a desire to play a role in public life and, if possible, try to find answers to the economic and political problems that confronted Britain in the 1970s. By seeking the wider application of ideas that he had developed when running his own company, and by helping or funding others, Vinson believed he could make a useful contribution in reversing Britain's economic and political decline. His enormously practical nature, great energy and infectious enthusiasm meant that there was no shortage of such requests; he was quite clearly a man who could make things happen – and he remains so even in his eighties.

As a young businessman, he had concluded that free enterprise was by far the best means to generate wealth and that the increasing scope of the state in seeking to own, regulate or control economic activity was inimical to economic growth and to liberty. He had come to appreciate that the market order was important in ensuring the existence of multiple sources of patronage for the artist, social reformer and inventor. And he also concluded that the wider ownership of wealth was essential if both its material and non-material benefits were to be more widely understood. His desire to ensure the wider diffusion of economic power was to remain a lifelong preoccupation.

Recognising that the radical policies needed to reverse Britain's decline could not be introduced without a fundamental change to the prevailing intellectual climate, Vinson assisted those engaged in an attempt to reverse the direction of political and economic thought in this country. He was invited to join the board of the Institute of Economic Affairs (IEA), which, under the leadership of Ralph Harris and Arthur Seldon, was to acquire a justified reputation as the most successful free-market think tank in history, helping to fund it at a time when money was in short supply. Twenty years later he was chairman for seven years and he has supported it throughout his lifetime. The IEA transformed the climate of economic opinion in Britain and beyond. Sir Alastair Burnet, editor of *The Economist* and a prominent neo-Keynesian, offered first-hand testimony of the process of how intellectual conversion was carried out:

> They came it seemed like spies in the night ... They were polite, even courteous, plainly intelligent fellows who enjoyed an argument. Only after a bit did it become apparent that they usually won their arguments. The well-drilled ranks of us Keynesians began to suffer uncomfortable casualties. The Butskellite regiments, entrenched in the ministries and universities, had severe butchers' bills. The intellectual concussion caused by the IEA conducted by Ralph Harris and Arthur Seldon ... upon the body politic and economic was cumulative and, eventually, decisive.

Vinson went on to help Margaret Thatcher and Keith Joseph found the Centre for Policy Studies (CPS) which took the arguments for the market economy more directly into the political arena, playing a major role in its activities. Recognising the centre's role in changing the direction of modern British political history, Mrs Thatcher said later: 'The Centre for Policy Studies was where our Conservative revolution began.' When Vinson resigned as the centre's honorary treasurer in 1980, Thatcher acknowledged that its achievements would not have been possible without his involvement.

As chairman of one of the CPS study groups, Vinson was directly responsible for proposals resulting in reforms that enabled company employees to take their pensions with them without penalty when changing jobs; he can also take credit for the ideas behind Pension Equity Plans (PEPs), as well as for the Enterprise Allowance scheme, which gave financial support to unemployed people to start their own businesses. Many Cabinet ministers have left office without achieving nearly as much.

Despite his growing influence and contribution to public life over four decades, and his elevation to the peerage in 1984, Vinson's name remains largely unknown to the public. This is partly because he does not seek the limelight and does not relish being continually in the public eye, and partly because – although offered a junior ministerial post, which he turned down – he has not held elected office. It is also a reflection of the fact that much of his time, as well as a great deal of his personal wealth, has been expended on helping others without seeking attention for himself. Nigel Vinson occasionally moves from centre stage in this account of his achievements because so much of what he has done

has been accomplished through mobilising others, supporting them, motivating them and doing all he can to ensure
that their contributions were acknowledged and rewarded.

Those he has helped have included not just think tanks,
but pressure groups, campaign bodies, charities, libertarian
causes (although he is not a libertarian in the accepted sense
of the term), organisations promoting the arts and crafts,
educational projects, wildlife protection groups (including
those for salmon stocks in the North Sea and the survival
of songbirds), as well as support for writers, scholars and
numerous other individuals. As with most good deeds, the
result has been a ripple effect as the consequences of his
actions have extended far beyond the original recipients.
Since Vinson has targeted his charitable giving wisely, the
impact of his generosity has been beneficial as well as per-
vasive. Although running into the millions, it is difficult to
quantify the extent of his philanthropy in financial terms:
he has never seen the point in adding up the sums he has
given to charitable and political causes, or the still larger
sum he has raised for such purposes from others.

In the Lords, Vinson established a reputation as a highly
conscientious, independent-minded Conservative peer with
a deep understanding of the problems of industry, rang-
ing from small firms to nationalised industries, as well as
an acute awareness of the unintended consequences of

regulation – the result of his directorships of the British Airports Authority and the Barclays main board.

Increasing scepticism about the value of Britain's membership of the European Union, for which he had voted in the 1975 referendum, led him to put down a series of questions about the costs of EU membership. By the time of the Maastricht Treaty in 1992, he had concluded that the economic and political costs of membership were excessive and that the very nature of the European project meant that it could never be fully democratically accountable. As chairman of the Better Off Out Group from 2008–11, he warned in August 2012 that, unless the Tory leadership took steps to repatriate powers from Brussels, he would resign the Tory whip and join UKIP. He also funded a serious study by Ian Milne to provide a rigorous cost benefit analysis of UK membership.

The wide diversity of Nigel Vinson's interests is the consequence of an innate sense of the fitness of things and an instinct, almost a reflex action, to seek solutions the moment he recognises a problem. As those who know him well have observed, he is constitutionally incapable of ignoring problems if he believes that he can make a contribution to their resolution – irrespective of whether the problem in question lies in the field of economic policy or in the social life of the rural community of Northumberland, in which he lives.

Some of the many public tasks he took on because he was asked to do so, and because he judged them worthwhile, have included the directorship of the Queen's Silver Jubilee Appeal, the chairmanship of the Crafts Council of Great Britain and the chairmanship of the Rural Development Commission (RDC), a role for which his love of the countryside and his understanding of small enterprises enabled him to bring new life and hope to rural communities by sweeping away restrictions on economic activity. In each case he refused payment, explaining that he believed those who could afford to do so should take on public service without pay.

His increasingly influential role in public life has been combined with farming and family interests, to which he brought the same drive and focus.

Nigel Vinson can take pride in having been one of the first Thatcherites – but Thatcherites come in different varieties. He is apt to take issue with those who talk or write about the market economy as if it were an entirely impersonal matter that functions irrespective of wider social factors and the moral climate. The only impersonal aspect of the market order, he points out, is price mechanism. Otherwise it is entirely a matter of human interaction, its great virtue lying in its sensitivity to changing human preferences. But he has always been at pains to stress that if the market is to work efficiently, it depends on trust – which in turn depends upon the moral conduct of individuals – and that markets, like humans, are never perfect.

Asked to explain the key to good business management and getting the best out of people, he told a journalist:

> Human nature is naturally helpful. I have always believed in two things: first that most people are intrinsically nice and they want to be so; and that if you treat others as you would wish to be treated yourself, then it makes the world go round. A philosophy as old as time.

He reflected further:

> I was born lucky – too young for the last war and too old for the next – into a well-off family during a period of unprecedented economic growth – and had drummed into me early that there are obligations that go with privilege and the blessing of good health, once called *noblesse oblige*.

Nigel Vinson's philosophy springs from a strongly religious background, both at home and at school – and, as this book reveals, he has been deeply influenced by it.

He would, however, describe himself as a 'partly doubtful'

Christian – unable to accept the virgin birth, believing that Christ was possibly more of a Messiah than the Son of God, and unpersuaded about an afterlife. Even so, he embraces – and has attempted to promote – Christian morality throughout his life, 'because it brings a hugely important moral framework and social cohesion to society. Science can never have an explanation as to where the energy of the universe comes from' – so he believes we should be in awe of, and give thanks for, the beauty of the earth and the miracle of a possibly God-given existence.

During the battle of political ideas that was waged in the 1970s and early '80s, some may have been impatient with the reiteration of Vinson's 'do as you would be done by' moral philosophy. Forty years on, following the banking crisis and reduced public confidence in almost every national institution, his insistence that economic outcomes are significantly influenced by the moral conduct of individuals is less easily dismissed. Moreover, if Vinson's approach to political and economic issues had been more widely shared, it is arguable that there would have been no need for Tory politicians to engage in an inappropriate exercise to rebrand the party's image.

This biography tells the story of a man whose influence, both direct and indirect, has been considerably greater than is widely realised; one who was often ahead of the trend, who saw through fashionable shibboleths and who, in his own life, has fully lived up to his belief that economic arrangements work best when individuals behave decently towards one another.

CHAPTER 1

To the manor born

NETTLESTEAD PLACE IS a beautiful fourteenth-century manor house set in the valley of the River Medway, just where the river cuts its way through the Greensand Ridge. The site borders a prehistoric track that follows the south side of the crest of the Ridge and crosses the river by means of a ford. The house, which in its early days served as a monastery, is listed in the *Domesday Book*. It later became a grand family house, standing just a short distance from the small parish church of St Mary's, whose origins also go back to Saxon times and whose fifteenth-century stained glass windows depict angels bearing heraldic shields. The main wing of the house, aligned east–west, is the oldest part and contains the crypt built in 1180, with the fifteenth-century extension to its eastern end. In the early 1920s, the house was rescued from a state of chronic disrepair, having been relegated to the role of oast house for two centuries. Ronald Vinson, a gentleman farmer of Huguenot descent, purchased the house and commissioned the architect Percy Morley Horder, famous for his design of congregational churches and Lloyd George's house at Walton Heath, to restore and extend Nettlestead so that once again it could become a family home. The east wing was enlarged and other major changes included the addition of two chimneys. The basic design of the gardens included some ancient trees – most notably a walnut, reputed to be 700 years old, and a medlar tree, whose drooping arms spread 50 ft across, making it an ideal place for children to play hide-and-seek. A large stew pond containing carp was fed by a spring delivering 10,000 gallons of crystal clear water a day. This pond was preserved while a second, smaller pond was turned into a rose garden.

It was at Nettlestead Place that Nigel, the second son of Ronald Vinson by his second wife Bettina, was born on 27

January 1931. 'Born ten days early and been in a hurry ever since,' she said.

Set within its own farmland, the house, the church and the tithe barn situated just a short distance away were to remain in Nigel's mind's eye throughout his life. Sadly, the tithe barn, one of the finest in Kent, was destroyed in 1962 by a fire started by a careless smoker on a day when the gardens were on view to the public. Today, the house, which was sold by the Vinsons in 1976, is rented out for wedding receptions and the gardens are visited by a steady stream of horticulturists.

It would be something of an exaggeration to say that Nigel came into the world with a silver spoon in his mouth, although he and his brother Mark (born three and a half years earlier but tragically killed in a tractor accident aged thirty-five – before the days of safety roll bars) certainly enjoyed a privileged upbringing entirely free of care and want.

At an early age, Nigel learned to fish, ride and shoot and also developed a growing interest in the running of his father's farms. By the age of seven, he could milk a cow; unfortunately the application of his skills in the milking shed resulted in ringworm, which continued to trouble him for a year. He was given his first pony Dapples and has continued to ride, often on a daily basis, throughout his life.

Most British food at that time was domestically produced. Food prices were high and rose higher during the
Second World War. Rising farm income, combined with
inherited wealth, meant that the Vinsons lived well; it was
some time before Nigel realised the truth of his parents'
gentle reminders that not everyone was as fortunate. The
family, before the war changed such lifestyles, employed
five domestic staff including a butler, a housekeeper and
two maids, not counting Violet – nanny to Mark and Nigel.
Violet, the daughter of the Vinsons' farm manager, had
no formal training as a nanny but had been given the
job because she struck them as personable, hardworking,
conscientious and loving. The decision was a wise one.
As a small boy, Nigel came to adore Violet, who clearly
returned his affection – once describing him to others as
'born wise'. He used to query 'How can you walk through
a looking glass?' and 'How can they go to sea in a sieve?
They would sink'.

Violet kept a promise not to marry and to stay with
the family until her charge was settled at school. Nigel
remained in contact with Violet throughout her life,
visiting her regularly, and he never forgot her birthday.
For her part, Violet followed Nigel's success with huge
pride. When, in his thirties, Nigel confided to her his
difficulties in finding a suitable wife, Violet was hugely

sympathetic. Her daughter, Mrs Gillian Coppins, told me: 'I remember her saying that her deepest wish was for Nigel to find a wife and be present to help when they started a family.' This is exactly what happened. Thirty years later, Violet was on hand when Vonnie, Nigel's wife, gave birth to Bettina, the first of their three daughters, who was named after his mother. Nigel recalls Violet as always busy and productive, sewing, tidying, making jam or preserves; he was deeply dismayed when she died from a heart attack in 1975, aged sixty-five, while shelling peas.

An outdoor staff of four included three gardeners and a chauffeur who maintained the family's cars. These included a V8 Daimler which, he would be delighted to know, is as treasured today by a vintage car enthusiast as it was sixty years ago. He also serviced the generator, producing the 100-volt DC electricity on which the household relied entirely for energy, in common with those living in similar country houses.

Nigel and Mark sometimes speculated as to whether the main bedroom of the house, which was of Elizabethan origins and situated over the Norman crypt, was haunted – a view given substance by their stepbrother Kenneth's solemn declaration that he had seen a ghost. More than seventy years later, Nigel can recall that when the family dogs approached the room, disobeying the rule that they should not be allowed upstairs, their hackles stood on end. On a deeper and more serious level, he has often reflected upon the impact of being brought up in a beautiful and ancient house, one that had evolved over time in response to the needs of those who lived in it, and the influence this has had on his own attitudes towards life and politics.

Vinson Senior owned four farms – Nettlestead, Bow Hill, Barming and Beckett's on Romney Marsh – amounting in all to around 1,200 acres. It was an era of farm mechanisation and innovation, and Nigel's father was among the first to acquire a tractor, replacing the horses by 1937.

When unwell at the age of six, Nigel was taken by Violet to stay for a few days with Mr and Mrs Martin, the Vinsons' tenants at Beckett's Farm – on land once owned by Thomas Beckett – in the hope that a change of scenery would restore his health. The farmhouse, which still stands, is 200 yards from Fairfield Church, made famous by Kipling's poem 'Brookland Road':

> O, Fairfield Church is water-bound
> From autumn to the spring;
> But it shall turn to high hill-ground
> Before my bells do ring.

Nigel recalls that to reach the church it was necessary to walk along a causeway over marshland which, as Kipling had pointed out, was often flooded despite being drained by ancient dykes. On arrival at the church, the family would file into one of the box pews where, as a way of encouraging him to remain silent during the sermon, he was permitted to play with his favourite train.

Much more satisfactory from his point of view were the fishing trips when he accompanied Farmer Martin to the dykes, a haven for wildlife of all kinds. These teemed with eels and carp, some said to be more than a hundred years old. On one such expedition, the two of them caught ten carp which were placed in a dustbin prior to their transfer to the garden pond at Nettlestead. On another occasion he recalls being dragged closer and closer to the water's edge by a giant eel on the end of his fishing line – an experience that was sufficiently frightening to a six-year-old to put him off his new hobby for several years.

Another childhood experience at Beckett's that remained firmly in his memory concerned the farm's shepherd, known locally as Old Addie, who appeared to be as old as time itself. Nigel watched as lambs were pushed into the shed in which Old Addie sat alone. What Nigel wanted to know from Violet was why it was that the lambs, part of a magnificent herd of Romneys, came to emerge hopping.

It was only later that he grasped the correct explanation – namely that Old Addie's jaws and teeth provided a quicker and more efficient method of castration than the sharpest knife!

As a young but increasingly knowledgeable observer of farming methods, Nigel witnessed farm horses being replaced by machines. He was a fan of both: he loved riding, but was also fascinated by machinery and wanted to know how it worked. From his father, who was recognised as the best shot in Kent – some said in England – he learned how to shoot and to fish. With his brother and local friends, he messed about on the boat that the family kept on the Medway, climbed ladders to pick cherries, and roamed freely over the farmland and the surrounding countryside without restriction and without constantly being told to be careful or not take risks.

In the immediate pre-war period, there were holidays at Lenzerheide in Switzerland – black tie at dinner and orchestras throughout – and visits to the Brux estate in Aberdeenshire, which provided exceptional opportunities to fish on the Don and shoot (Nigel was not attracted to the idea of shooting deer and turned down opportunities to do so). One holiday in this period took them to Salcombe where they were rowed out to see the wreck of one of the last grain clippers, the *Herzogin Cecilie*, who broke her back on the bar at night, having just achieved one of the fastest runs on record – eighty-six days from Australia.

His curiosity about the practical aspects of running a farm often centred on the activities of Tilsley, their carpenter, who patiently explained the rudiments of his craft, and to whose workshop the boy was a constant visitor. Years later, he could recall how Tilsley constructed one of the first carts to be drawn by a tractor, an early example of hybrid transport.

Learning by watching the farm craftsmen imbued in him an ingrained understanding of the time and effort needed to make things. This not only benefitted him in business but reinforced his comprehension of the intrinsic worth put into craftsmanship, both old and new – a judgement he was to value throughout his life.

Not even his parents' determination to see that he was properly educated could destroy the sense of freedom and innocent inquiry he then enjoyed. Miss Dyson, a visiting governess, called on a daily basis to give lessons, where he was joined by three other local boys – one of whom, Mark Stratton, remained a great friend and they were even still fishing together in their eighties on the Grimersta, near Stornoway. Miss Dyson, an inspiring teacher, did everything she could to feed the hungry minds of her pupils and was popular with all her charges.

Nigel's mother, the daughter of a GP, had been one of the first female medical students at Edinburgh but she gave up her studies to marry Ronald Vinson after the death of Constance, his first wife, during the pneumonia epidemic that followed the First World War. This had left him to bring up his three young sons – Kenneth, his twin Anthony (later killed in the war when piloting a bomber over Dresden) and John – but they all came to love and admire their stepmother. Although Bettina, by marrying early, was never able to achieve her ambition to qualify as a doctor, her sons' occasional childhood illnesses provided her with the opportunity to apply her skills, a role in which, according to Nigel, she greatly excelled. The epitaph, subscribed by the old people's home to which she gave ten years' dedicated attention, read: *Her loving kindness endeared her to many.*

A voracious reader who consumed three books a week, Bettina supplemented the formal education provided by the incomparable Miss Dyson by reading to her sons from the classics. Kipling was a particular favourite and Nigel acquired a great regard for what he describes as 'the poet's perceptive common sense'. Conan Doyle was another. Despite his love of Kipling, he gradually developed an indifference towards novels, based on an instinctive belief that there were more worthwhile things to read and that real-life stories were far more interesting. He preferred to read biography and travel books.

For much of the time however, Nigel – a sensitive child – was left to his own devices, with his mother devoting much of her time to his brother Mark, who suffered from poor health. Vinson Senior had already fathered four sons by the time of Nigel's birth, and hoped for a daughter; he burst into tears when it was another boy. It was perhaps this, coupled with a growing incompatibility with his wife, that caused him to give little time to his youngest child.

The lack of parental attention during Nigel's early years – which he attributes to the effects of the war – was deeply felt, resulting in a sense of inadequacy and a vulnerability that was partly overcome by his natural self-confidence (a paradox only those very close to him have glimpsed). In later life, he was determined that his own children would never be sidelined in such a way. His childhood was also clouded by an increasing awareness that his parents' marriage was far from ideal and that the differences between them were growing. Nevertheless, with limitless opportunities to develop his love of country sports and to indulge a growing interest in how things were made and assembled, with local friends as well as domestic staff and farm workers for company and with Violet to care for him and to take pride in his progress there were many compensations.

Shortly after his eighth birthday Nigel was sent to Brambletye, the family's traditional preparatory school at East Grinstead, to which his elder brother and stepbrothers had all gone. Thirty years later, he was to become a governor of the school.

In a diary kept to record Nigel's progress during the years 1939–54, his mother wrote: 'Went off to Brambletye for first term: so brave at leaving … so self-possessed and good.'

His earliest impressions of the school centred on the beauty of the surroundings. Fifty years later he wrote: 'Brambletye was set in the most beautiful grounds and I remember clearly playing marbles near the underground gym and lying under giant oak trees watching a horde of caterpillars letting themselves down on silken ropes from the branches above.'

An entry in his mother's diary dated March 1939 reads:

> Getting on so well. Happy and full of fun. Particularly good at football and rather devoted to Violet. Writes to her weekly … determined and self-possessed and self-reliant. Very interested in everything practical and good with his hands. Extremely affectionate to a very few. Doesn't like correction, resents punishment. Full of life, fun, jokes and laughter.

Elsewhere in her diary she recorded that Nigel loved being read to and was subsequently reading books that were very advanced for his age. He is deeply indebted to his mother for the thirst of knowing the how and why, which has remained throughout his life.

The subsequent recollections of Nigel's school friends confirm the truth of his mother's observations, while calling into question the accuracy of her tribute to his prowess on the football field. Indifference to ball games, largely due to debilitating hay fever, deflected his energy to the school ranges, where he became a good shot, and remains so into his eighties.

School life was not perhaps quite as idyllic as his earlier years. In his view, those who declare that school days are the happiest days of their lives 'must live pretty miserable lives thereafter'.

Nigel recalled later:

> Many boys used to say how they longed to get back from their holidays so they could play sport and see their friends. To Mark and me it was the other way around. There was always something to do or see at home, whether it was boating on the Medway, watching massive old cherry tree stumps being blown up by dynamite to make way for replanting, helping to

make butter, taking honey from the bees, seeing runner beans salted down in crocks for the winter, eggs being preserved in isinglass and fruit bottled in kilner jars – all before the age of home refrigeration. We were left alone on the pond in boats, to climb trees or to wander along the rail line that passed our house. I never remember my parents saying that we couldn't do any of that because it was too dangerous. Human beings have fear and caution bred into their bones – and learn to assess risk at a very early age. Over-protection can impair this process – and spoil much innocent fun.

Brambletye was, and is, a very good school. Although discipline was tough by contemporary standards – with even minor misdemeanours being punished by blows from a fives bat – the teachers, who placed great emphasis on the development of character, were mostly kind and dedicated. The quality of teaching was high, although this later became patchy, as staff left to perform war service and it was difficult to find replacements. As a consequence, senior boys were given a role in helping to run the school and enjoyed much greater freedom than was to be the case at Pangbourne, his next school. Later, he recalled that so much stress was placed on adherence to a moral code emphasising the importance of owning up to one's misdemeanours that, on more than one occasion, he confessed to misdemeanours he was uncertain of having committed.

> There was an aura of trust about life at Brambletye.
> Anything anybody said was automatically taken as the
> truth. Nobody appeared to say anything that wasn't
> the truth, and this perhaps has led me to trust every-
> one, until given reason not to … A deep underlying
> religious morality gave an unexpressed, wholesome
> atmosphere to life at the school. Perhaps this golden
> age of sensible levels of discipline helped instil moral
> certainty … John Blencowe [the headmaster] had a
> great sense of calling, and was also imbued with a for-
> midable sense of duty … Nobody talked about rights.
> Duties and obligations were taken for granted.

Nigel arrived for his first term at Brambletye carrying a
tool box, and later deeply impressed his contemporaries by
constructing a crystal set, based on the design of a friend's.
'It was the start of a hugely rewarding hobby that led to an
understanding of electronics and radio communication,
which was of inestimable value to me when I was building
up my plastics business.'

Among his first impressions of the school was that
of being kept awake in the dormitory by a boy called

Peter Wedderburn-Ogilvy, who was to become a lifelong friend. Wedderburn-Ogilvy was suffering from acute mastoiditis, recovery from which was slow and painful prior to the introduction of penicillin. Nigel recalls: 'Miss Andrews, the school nurse, came regularly to comfort him; a change from her normal duties, which included knocking on the door of the landing WC and asking "Who's in there, and why?".'

Class attendance was frequently reduced by infectious diseases, which were far more prevalent than today. At one stage, Nigel was the only boy in his form who had not been consigned to the sick bay with whooping cough. 'So I coughed myself silly and was eventually allowed to join them. To this day, I do not know whether I really had whooping cough or not.'

In the weeks leading to the Munich Agreement, Nigel was dispatched to Scotland with his nanny, only to be pulled out of the train at King's Cross to return home when war was averted. The following year, Nigel, Mark and nanny found themselves at the Aberfeldy Hotel in Scotland and on 3 September 1939 they listened with fellow guests to the radio announcement of the outbreak of war, whereupon some guests burst into tears. Shortly afterwards they returned home when it became clear that there was no immediate sign Kent was being targeted.

Following the opening of hostilities, the school was evacuated to Lee Abbey near Lynton on the north Devon coast, where the classrooms consisted of converted garages, the dormitories were unheated and the conditions Spartan. This allowed lessons to continue in relative safety but also meant that pupils did not see their parents for ten, twelve or even fourteen weeks at a time.

Nigel picked things up quickly and finished top of the third form at the end of his first year. Regrettably, however, this led to his being over-promoted to the Remove (or fifth form), owing to the disruption when the school was evacuated to Lee Abbey, thus skipping the fourth year form into which all his friends went. This resulted in a huge setback in his confidence as he went from being top dog to bottom dog. Having, in effect, missed a year's schooling as a result, he totally failed to maintain his earlier progress. Nigel also found himself the victim of occasional bullying from older boys. In retrospect, he is inclined to the view that this may have done him some good since it taught him to be sympathetic later in life when he encountered misfortune in others.

Nigel's principal memories of Lee Abbey were of missing his family, of war debris being washed up on the sands and of being restricted to one Mars bar a week as a result of wartime rationing.

Our diet was adequate – but only just. I can still recall
the craving for chocolate and sugar – which was not
just a spoiling treat but necessary because of its energy-
giving properties. I think we were allowed 6d a week
pocket money, which bought a bar of chocolate prior to
heavy rationing in 1944, after which they were a rarity.

When my father sent by train a huge 20lb box of
cherries from our farm at Bow Hill, it was consumed
within minutes, as if by locusts.

As the German blitz intensified through 1941 the boys
could hear the drone of German bombers trying to reach
Bristol, followed by a huge sense of excitement when one
was shot down.

Nigel recalls being woken at night by mines hitting the
beach below with explosions that sent shudders round
the main school building. A memorable day was when the
boys heard a German bomber that ran out of fuel and
crashed into the hills above the school, an incident
followed by trophy collecting the pieces of aircraft wreck-
age: 'Schoolboys love spy theories. The twinkling lights
in the woods, and sometimes out to sea, made us think
that there were spies operating in this corner of England.
Perhaps there were. Masters were endlessly regaled with
boys' reports of the flashings of secret lights at night.'

In common with his school friends, Nigel greatly missed home, but he found some compensation. The boys were allowed to roam the grounds, which covered 500 acres, although they were barred from Lovers Leap, a dangerous precipice from which, it was rumoured, the love-stricken leapt to their deaths: 'The outdoor life at Lee Abbey was always such a joy, using chairs to toboggan down grassy slopes, building huts, exploring the woods and cliffs, going to the beach and picking up the detritus of war – hundreds of gas masks, hoses and piles of timber from torpedoed cargo ships.'

An early sign of Nigel's sense of independence came when he absented himself from art class in order to listen to radio news of the war:

> When Mr Wilson [a senior master] asked me why I had made myself absent to listen to the radio I said that I thought what was happening in France was more important than ten minutes of an art lesson. He turned his back and walked out of the door without saying anything. So he must have agreed!

Nigel also found himself struggling to learn French and Latin grammar. Why couldn't one begin by learning to *speak* a foreign tongue, just as one had learned one's own language as a child, before going on to learn grammar? What was the point of struggling to learn a dead language? Being forced to decline verbs at the age of eight just seemed wrong.[1] For the first time, he reflected on the fact that those with the ability to influence one's happiness and wellbeing are not necessarily infallible, even when they have one's best interests at heart. His response to the problems he was experiencing in making academic progress was a typically practical one: he asked to sit in the front row of the class. This resulted in some modest progress, but did not turn him into a linguist. He was far from being a rebel, but at a relatively early age he was developing a sense of independence, a reluctance to accept uncritically the infallibility of those in authority and a desire to make decisions for himself, which later on was to grow into a desire to be his own boss.

Peter Wedderburn-Ogilvy remembers Nigel as a leading member of the school's Dramatic Entertainment Society, which, he says, was essentially a front for schoolboy larking-about and never produced anything much in the way of entertainment.

---

1 To this day he argues passionately that the system of language teaching at that time was wrong. He believes that children should first enjoy speaking simple sentences in a foreign language before mastering the grammar, just as they did in their own language. The last thing they need at the age of eight is to know the past pluperfect of verbs – few people know this, even in their own language.

Nigel's own recollection is that the Dramatic Society's output was not as modest as his old school friend remembers and that he greatly enjoyed performing the tasks of stage manager, a role that he was later to perform at Pangbourne.

Wedderburn-Ogilvy recalls:

> Nigel was not brilliant at school and never made it into the top form but his career serves as a marvellous demonstration that school is incapable of teaching you the things that really matter in life – enterprise, management skills, leadership, initiative, and get-up-and-go – all of which Nigel possessed in abundance.
>
> My other recollection of him is that he was always messing around with radios, and had already established a reputation among his contemporaries as a brilliant engineer.

Returning home during the school holidays was like arriving in a war zone. Nigel later recorded:

> Arriving home in Kent was like returning to the front line. Initially, when the village air raid siren sounded we trooped to the underground shelter, practised wearing our gas masks and waited for something to happen.

Life went on: as the war progressed we got more adventurous and stood outside to watch. The sky was criss-crossed with searchlights picking out planes for anti-aircraft to shoot. My brother was nearly killed when the nose-cone from a shell missed him by inches as he was feeding his guinea pigs; we had great fun digging it out the next morning. The Blitz intensified: at night we could see London burning 30 miles away, the whole sky ablaze like a red sunset. The German bombers, protected by their own fighters, came over in formations of twenty-four – a throbbing ominous drone. A young Spitfire pilot was billeted with us for six months – then one night he was killed. At its climax, over a hundred planes were shot down, ending German air superiority and saving Britain from invasion. We witnessed the disintegration of dozens of aircraft – machines and men – twisting to earth through a chaotic tumult of machine gun fire and screaming engines.

Returning from Devon at the start of the school holidays I saw seven enemy bombers shot down, the pilot of one plunging to the ground, his parachute blazing. Two years later I narrowly missed being killed when a flying bomb skimmed Nettlestead and dropped a short distance away.

He later wrote to a friend: 'Deep in my memory there is the sight of London burning – a red glow across the whole horizon, a scarlet sunset of fire across huge swathes of our capital city.'

Looking back, Vinson believes that by demonstrating life's fragility, the war strengthened his desire to achieve something in life and also encouraged a practical *will it help us win the war?* mentality, which stayed with him.

His choice of public school – Pangbourne Naval College in Berkshire – was dictated partly by his dislike of Latin, which was not compulsory as it was at nearly all public schools at the time, and partly by a short-lived desire to follow his uncle who was a Surgeon Captain in the Royal Navy. Many had commented how well suited he seemed when wearing a sailor's uniform aged six for that same uncle's wedding. In such ways are big decisions taken!

On a visit to Pangbourne he had been impressed by the school's workshop and the activities of its science society, of which he was later to become chairman. His happiest days appear to have been spent building radios; he also played a leading role in arranging the light and sound systems and organising the production as stage manager of the school's drama society.

John Whitmore met Nigel on their first day at Pangbourne and, despite different interests, became a lifelong friend. John was good at languages and later took classes in Latin with the aim of going up to Cambridge, an ambition he later fulfilled. Nigel continued to express dislike for the priority given to dead languages and the way in which they were taught at school. Both quickly abandoned their ambition to join the Royal Navy, realising that a career in the services would necessarily involve a loss of independence and the acceptance of discipline in small matters as well as large. Nigel also suffered from sea sickness:

> We both fell out of love with the idea of a life in the services when we realised that it would involve subjecting ourselves to many unnecessary rules and regulations and being confined to half an acre of tossing metal for weeks on end, with nothing to see but the sea.

More than sixty years later, Whitmore, who went into the family tanning company before becoming a successful fruit farmer, recalls the inventiveness displayed by his friend in finding excuses to avoid playing cricket and rugby, as well as his reputation for being able to build and repair radios from an early age. He remembers that both bridled against authority and that Nigel was not timid about disagreeing with the masters. 'Nigel was never shy about making his views known. I would say that we were both more rebellious than most and, as non-conformists, were not always on good terms with the management.'

Despite his display of independence, Nigel was appointed cadet captain (senior prefect) during his final year, during which time he learned an important lesson about the nature of authority as well as the need to exercise it with humour and common sense.

These insights were afforded to Nigel during one of the school's periodic anti-smoking campaigns, when a boy called Maggs, who was known to be a heavy smoker, was called before Rear Admiral Oliphant, the Pangbourne headmaster, after a complaint from a teacher.

The headmaster told the boy:

> Maggs, I understand that Mr Sykes visited the Piggeries behind the classroom block at five minutes to eleven, and subsequently saw you go into the Piggeries at three minutes past eleven at which point he immediately revisited them and found this packet of twenty-five cigarettes on the floor, which hadn't been there before. What have you to say?

Maggs replied: 'Not guilty, sir, I only buy them in hundreds.'

Rear Admiral Oliphant replied: 'Maggs, of course you are telling the truth! Case dismissed.'

Nigel repeated this anecdote when, as a member of the House of Lords and a highly successful entrepreneur, he returned to the school nearly four decades later, on 12 July 1986, to deliver the Founders' Day Address.

> As you can imagine the boys worshipped the head-master because he trusted people. He treated them as equal, though different, and so people trusted him in return. That incident, which provided a marvel-lous example of true leadership, taught me more than words can say. As for Maggs, he may not have known the aphorism, 'Truth is more important than conse-quence,' but he certainly practised it.

Despite Nigel's decision not to embark on a naval career or to lay serious claim to any of the school's academic hon-ours, Pangbourne's head wrote in his final school report: 'I am very sorry to lose him. He will, I know, always bring credit to his family and his school.'

The school's director of studies, Kenneth Topliss, added: 'He is lively and intelligent and will do well in any profes-sion to which he puts his hand. He has done more than he realises ... and has been very helpful to me.'

In his final exams, Nigel achieved five credits and a pass – sufficient to win him a place at London University

– but the lack of a Classics qualification ruled out an Oxbridge place, a fact to which he had already happily reconciled himself. By that stage, he had already concluded that practical business experience would provide a better springboard to success, and the fulfilment of his dream of being his own boss, than would a university course.

At seventeen, while waiting to be called up for national service, he went to South Africa. Having travelled out as cheaply as possible – steerage on a small merchant ship – he spent his first night at Cape Town in a seamen's hostel. Awaking the next morning, he could not understand why all twenty-three men in the dormitory where he had slept the night looked virtually identical – until he discovered they were a boatload of inbred Tristan de Cunies, direct descendants of the mutineers on the *Bounty*. He subsequently toured South Africa with a friend in a secondhand car, spending his eighteenth birthday in the Kruger National Park before going to Mozambique and what was then Rhodesia – a journey of 2,000 miles conducted without much thought for personal safety. He visited and was immensely impressed by Lutyens's memorial to Cecil Rhodes and its epitaph:

His immense and brooding spirit shall quicken and control
Living he was the land and dead his soul shall be her soul.

Many of Nigel's contemporaries found national service an irritating distraction from the pursuit of career goals, but his own army service provided the opportunity to travel and interact with those from very different social backgrounds. Following the example of an uncle who had been a colonel in the regular army, Nigel chose to join the West Kent Regiment. After undergoing initial training at the regiment's headquarters at Shorncliffe near Folkestone, Private Vinson was selected to sit the War Office examination for officers, which, at that time, involved written assessment as well as practical tests.

After passing the exam, Vinson, now aged eighteen and a half, was sent for officer training at Eaton Hall outside Chester. He was subsequently posted to the Queen's Own Infantry Regiment, then based in Mogadishu. He did not know where Mogadishu was but, having consulted his atlas and discovered that it was the capital of what was then Italian Somalia, he prepared for a lengthy sea voyage to his posting. Arriving in Port Said on the first stage of his journey he learned that there would be a three-week delay before the next ship left for Somalia and that, during this period, he would be posted to the army's headquarters at 3 Brigade as transport officer.

In his new role, Vinson's positive attitude evidently impressed his commanding officer, one Brigadier Hexham, who telephoned the War Office to request that he should be allowed to retain the services of Second Lieutenant Vinson as his ADC. It was a change of plan that met with Vinson's full approval since he concluded that duties at Brigade Headquarters would be more stimulating than a posting to Mogadishu where regimental life, with its emphasis on heavy drinking and mess-room camaraderie, held limited appeal. Moreover, whenever 3 Brigade went on manoeuvres, the task of transport officer was combined with that of intelligence officer, whose role included plotting a 200-mile route through the Sinai Desert with the aid of a sun compass in temperatures of 100°F. Until they got to know him, Brigade members may have had private reservations about being led through the blistering heat of the Sinai by a fresh-faced teenager who looked even younger than his years. But, after successfully directing the Brigade on its manoeuvres from deep in the desert to within half a mile of Base Camp on his first exercise, they acknowledged that as fresh-faced teenage officers went, Vinson was a good deal better than he looked.

On one such trip, in a remote part of the desert, Vinson came across a 2 million-year-old petrified forest, a small part of which he took home and continues to use as a paper weight. Leisure time was split between visiting Egypt's ancient sites, swimming in the Suez Canal and sunbathing.

Army life was not without its occasional embarrassments. Sent by his commanding officer to Cairo to meet General (later Sir) Geoffrey Bourne on a tour of inspection, Lieutenant Vinson placed his jacket on the rear seat of the glass-partitioned staff car only to find later that it had been stolen at a checkpoint as the vehicle had slowed. Acutely embarrassed that he should be arriving incorrectly dressed to meet the most senior officer he had ever encountered, Vinson explained what had occurred, but the General, who had only one arm, made light of the incident:

> As we went through the checkpoints on our return journey to Brigade Headquarters, the General would put his one arm out of the window and roar: 'Hang on to your luggage!' It was a marvellous way of putting at ease a young subaltern who had dropped a real clanger, and by example it taught me a great deal.

As demob day approached, Nigel began to think about his first steps in building a career, but, on returning home, all his tentative plans had to be placed on hold when a decision was made to extend national service by a further six months following the outbreak of war in Korea. Lieutenant Vinson was instructed to report as weapons training officer back at Shorncliffe Barracks, a posting that enabled him to drive home every weekend to Nettlestead in a newly acquired Ford 8 car. It was during this period that his desire to become his own boss and to chart his own course in life turned into a firm resolve.

CHAPTER 2

Walking the ship

THE ORIGINS OF Plastic Coatings, the company which would make Nigel Vinson a wealthy man and provide the foundation of his subsequent successes, can be traced to a visit made to a small plastics factory by his school science society, of which he was the keen chairman.

> When I saw what this factory did, I thought to myself: 'This technology is a piece of cake,' so I went back

and read a few books on the subject which confirmed
my belief that what I really wanted to do in life was
to have a business of my own in the plastics industry.

Later on, he discovered that starting and running a small
business, far from being a piece of cake, was an all-consuming
preoccupation, especially during the worrying stages of its
development. The real value of the school visit was that
it convinced him that plastics was a growth industry of
the future and consequently offered exciting and rewarding opportunities for any young and ambitious man of
practical disposition, even those whose only professional
training had been national service.

Many years later, at a seminar on the role of the entrepreneur run by the IEA in 1980, he explained:

> I always had a deep ambition to be self-employed – to
> be my own boss – or, as I would put it now, to be free of
> other people's power. After national service I weighed
> up my prospects and, in place of university, decided to
> learn about plastics, since I believed that by joining a
> growth industry I would at least stand a chance of grow-
> ing with it. Probably this was the only rational decision
> I took, and a vital one, because the plastics industry
> has grown at a 14 per cent compound rate for years.

Shortly after completing national service, Vinson, then aged twenty, went to the 1951 *Daily Mail* Ideal Home Exhibition, armed with references from school and the army, in the hope of identifying a plastics company that would give him a job and an entry into his chosen industry. Ex-Lieutenant Vinson was well dressed, politely spoken, keen to learn, self-confident and brimming with enthusiasm – qualities that have not diminished with the passing of the years. His evident ambition and commitment so impressed Tony Anselm, the boss of Creators Ltd (a small Woking-based plastics company), that he offered Nigel a job on the spot. Terms and conditions were settled and it was agreed that he should start the following Monday. But when he arrived for his first day of work, he was told that there had been a change of heart: there was no longer a job for him, and it was just unfortunate that a letter saying this apparently had not reached him in time. Vinson expressed huge disappointment. Anselm responded by offering him a job on the production line. Other public school-educated, ex-national service officers, conscious of the lower status that this new offer entailed, might well have declined. Vinson accepted with enthusiasm, starting work on the bench then and there on a wage of £4 a week.

'Many of my contemporaries thought it most unusual that I should want to go into industry. Far from being disappointed, it was exactly what I wanted. I have always enjoyed making things and the job gave me first-hand knowledge of how plastics goods were made,' he said later.

After several months it was realised that, while his spelling was far from perfect, the company could take advantage of the fact that this highly personable young man was capable of writing and speaking persuasively in clear English. He was therefore transferred to the sales department. In his new role, he learned about the commercial aspects of the company's affairs and, much more importantly, made a discovery that he would use to good advantage: the firm frequently received requests that it could not meet to cover metal items with a plastic coating rather than rubber. Having reflected on the matter, he concluded that, if more efficient systems were devised for this purpose, there would be a huge number of applications, with potential demand in home and industry. He observed that, in its basic simplicity, this idea had much in common with many other groundbreaking ideas for products and services. He wrote later:

> The reality is that good inventions and good ideas do not necessarily have to be complicated and expensive to be effective. Barbed wire transformed agriculture, the polythene bag made deep freezing feasible, the

chain-saw revolutionised tree felling. These relatively simple inventions, requiring no great research programme, have had as big an impact on society as carbon fibre.

At about the same time as Vinson was thinking about how his ideas might be put into practice, he was given £12,000 by his parents as part of the arrangements for their divorce. He approached his boss to suggest that they set up a jointly-owned company to develop the processes necessary to coat a variety of metal items with plastic. His boss's blunt response was that fifty/fifty companies never worked, and that, if he was really determined to go ahead with the idea, he should go away and start up by himself. This is exactly what Vinson did, remaining faithful to a promise not to poach work from his old company, but taking with him his secretary, Jean Ewans, who proved to be loyal and devoted to her boss beyond the call of duty – and would even stay on to help pack and dispatch the finished products immediately after her secretarial tasks were completed.

Vinson wanted to call his company Flexible Plastics, but, in order to meet the requirements of the registration process, settled for Durable Plastics. He had now acquired a partner, a friend called Ewan Blakely. Vinson was just twenty-one when Durable Plastics was registered on

18 September 1952, following a five-month search for suitable low-cost accommodation – a Nissen hut on the site of the old Friary Brewery in the middle of Guildford. The frustration he felt while searching for suitable premises made him aware that, apart from finance, this was a major obstacle in setting up a small business – an experience on which he would draw when he became chairman of the RDC nearly thirty years later.

The process he wished to develop involved dipping pre-heated metal items into liquid plastisols, withdrawing them after fifteen seconds and then reheating in order to cure the plastic coating, a procedure that took fifteen minutes from beginning to end. This was ideal for the purpose of coating plate racks (which previously displayed a tendency to rattle and fall apart) and also for making simple mouldings. Sixty years later, one of the first plate racks to be coated in this way remains in use in Vinson's kitchen – a clear sign that the process lived up to the claim made by the company's title.

The first order came from a Surrey-based company that produced air-sea rescue equipment and wanted plastic caps, which could be fitted to the end of whistles on plastic life vests, so that those struggling for survival in the water would have something to bite on. Priced at a penny each and with 20,000 to produce, the company was off to a promising start.

As a result of searching through trade magazines for items that had previously been coated or made in rubber, the company brought in sufficient new business to enable the recruitment of its first employee, an ex-NCO called Jim Poulter, who was hired as a result of an advertisement in a local newspaper. He stayed with the company at Guildford for the next forty years. A remarkably conscientious and able foreman, even to the extent that, one day, having just cycled 5 miles home at night, he thought he had forgotten to turn off the gas, so cycled back again – to find he had after all! When retired, he often came to stay with Nigel and Yvonne in Northumberland for a holiday.

At around this time, Vinson learned of a new German process of spraying powdered plastic onto metal and also grasped that the powders could be turned into fluid. The process of fluidisation – to give the process its technical term – was achieved through the use of a tank with a porous base that diffused the air and turned all above it – whether sand or plastic – into a mist, enabling metal items more easily and rapidly to be dipped. This discovery coincided with the introduction of polythene, which turned out to be the ideal coating for many items. These developments enabled Vinson to fulfil an order to supply Hoover with 5,000 wire hanger brackets per week for its washing machines – a major step forward in the growth of the company.

The order boosted confidence as well as income, but also presented a major challenge. By that stage, the gas and electricity supplies to the Nissen hut were running at full capacity and it was not clear how the heat required to dry 3,000 brackets would be created. But Vinson remembered an important principle – the principle of resistance heating that he had learned from Mr Beet, his physics master at Pangbourne. This holds that the degree of heating for a given electric current is proportional to the electrical resistance of the conductor and that, if the resistance is high, a large amount of heat can be generated. By applying this principle, heat was provided across the brackets using a fraction of the power requirements of a large oven.

Although the technical problems in meeting the Hoover order were successfully solved, the Nissen hut was now overcrowded. Luckily, two adjacent Nissen huts came on the market and were immediately snapped up along with a vacant warehouse.

Vinson's old school friend from Brambletye, Peter Wedderburn-Ogilvy, was an early visitor to the first of the Nissen huts that the company was to occupy: 'It was a fantastic Heath Robinson affair with bits of metal hanging from string attached to the ceiling, but there was a great sense of purpose and dynamism about the place. And soon the firm expanded into a second Nissen hut, and then another...'

Within three years the company was employing thirty people, after which it grew to 1,000 employees over the next seventeen years at some 20 per cent compound rate in turnover. Productivity over this time increased nine-fold as the process was refined and automated.

In 1956, just four years after its launch, the company moved to a purpose-built factory following the acquisition of two adjacent plots covering a three-quarter-acre site at Woodbridge Meadows in Guildford, on long leases from Guildford Council at a remarkably low ground rent.

> By 1955 we were bursting at the seams and, as good fortune would have it, Guildford Council had decided to develop an industrial estate adjacent to the Guildford Bypass. We were the first applicants and very welcome. We secured a 99-year lease for £640 – unindexed – and I couldn't believe our luck.

The new buildings, which took six months to complete, included offices, storage space and laboratories as well as production facilities.

A £14,000 loan to construct the new buildings came from the company's insurers Eagle Star, which Vinson was able to approach confident in the knowledge that the completed factory would be worth more than it cost. However, just two weeks before the move to the new factory in November 1956, the company suffered a setback when Vinson's partner, Ewan Blakely, and the firm's engineering foreman walked out to start their own company, poaching 20 per cent of its business.

> It was the worst possible moment for this to happen and it produced the kind of sickening feeling in the stomach that is not unknown to company bosses who find that their plans are put at risk by those who want to steal the business and run off and become entrepreneurs. But such was the flow of new business and the loyalty and commitment of the remaining staff that we went from strength to strength, while the new company prospered for a short while, and then collapsed.

But behind this apparent rapid success, Vinson told the author:

> It is not until you have run a small business that you realise the stress and constant anxiety that comes from having total responsibility for everything, and the nightmares you have that you will run out of orders and have no jobs for anybody by the end of the month. Fortunately, being in my twenties, I had little to lose and could always start again.

42

The new systems that Vinson and his growing team devised enabled a diverse range of household and industrial items – from draining racks for crockery and kitchen utensils to North Sea oil rigs, and from garden furniture to surgical instruments – to be covered with a variety of protective coatings including nylon, polythene and PVC. This system increasingly replaced painting and plating as a means of protecting metal against corrosion and wear, methods which were more expensive and less effective.

The construction in 1956 of a new production line, using parts of an airframe from an obsolete Brabazon aircraft that had been sold off as scrap, enabled the company to process items of increasing weight and size up to 5 metres in length. Acting as a kind of high-tech laundry for industry, large pieces of metalwork such as industrial pipes weighing several tonnes, could, for the first time, be cleaned and protectively coated much more rapidly than was previously possible.

Among the growing volume of heavy items were the lead ballast blocks contained in the hulls of Britain's nuclear submarines, which needed to be protected from corrosion. For security reasons, these were delivered at night, treated by a dedicated specialist team and returned again the following nightfall.

Domestic applications included the non-stick coatings

for frying pans and other cooking instruments, refrigerator shelves, washing machine baskets and window frames. Industrial applications included coatings for lighting and roadside columns, chemical pipework and tanks, rollers for paper-making machinery, agricultural equipment, seat-belt buckles, electronic components, metal furniture and office equipment, balustrades, confectionery moulds, machine tool parts, car and aircraft components, and even the railings around Hyde Park.

A huge order from an Italian company for the transparent coating of glass aerosol bottles (which would contain the glass if accidentally broken) presented a major practical problem. The order was on such a scale that it could have meant letting down existing customers. Displaying the characteristic ingenuity on which the company's success crucially depended, Vinson resolved the problem by instructing his engineering team to build a prototype production line that could be sold to the Italian firm so it could produce its own containers. It was the first of the company's major engineering sales, which were to develop substantially over the next decade. During the installation, Nigel learned that there are, in fact, dozens of different forms of Parma ham – but that it is a mistake to combine them with too much Chianti!

Vinson also impressed his colleagues with his ingenuity

when he devised a solution to a problem that occurred when liquid plastic was pumped under a vacuum. This was not a straightforward matter because the pumps used in the process sucked in air through the glands of their shafts, causing the liquid plastic to bubble. Numerous commercial pumps were tried without significant success. The answer, Vinson concluded, was to encase the entire pump in a vacuumed chamber, balancing the air pressure across the seals, thus avoiding the ingress of air that caused the bubbles. The end result was a transparent and completely bubble-free coating, representing another step forward in the company's record of technical innovation.

By the 1960s, three principal techniques were used: dipping into a tank of liquid; dipping into fine powder; and spraying. Exports to more than twenty countries included the machinery that the company's engineers and scientists, and Vinson himself, had developed in the company's new Equipment Division:

> The golden rule was never to sell any equipment until we had fully proven it on our own premises – thus saving many a nightmare when it came to providing after-sales service. This was something that the management failed to grasp after I left the company, and it cost them dearly.

In 1960, the firm changed its name to the more self-explanatory title of Plastic Coatings. Many of the products that they helped design for their customers were subsequently chosen by the Design Council and led to Vinson being invited to become chairman of their Selection Panel, opening the Design Council's annual meeting one year at the Royal Mint, and even being invited by the Hong Kong government to go out and advise on the setting-up of a design exhibition centre.

Demand for the company's services expanded hugely and, during the years that followed, factories were opened in Farnham, Surrey, at Winsford, Cheshire, in Kingswinford, Staffordshire, and at Harpenden, Hertfordshire.

While it is much more agreeable to expand the business than to contract it, promoting or recruiting the appropriate staff for the new division is always easier said than done. Will the job make the man? Will his wife move with him? Will he be able to cope with all the myriad concerns – sickness, absence, health and safety inspections, forward ordering – and above all keep the customers happy?

Shall I lease or buy the new factory? Is it more or less in the right place? – close enough to the shops to let the staff pop out at lunchtime? Shall we put the canteen out to a caterer or run it ourselves?

From the beginning Vinson had set a 'can-do' motivational tone – being among the first to arrive in the morning and among the last to leave and taking only two weeks' holiday, some of which was spent on service in the Territorial Army.

Friday evening at the Guildford factory concluded with a staff meeting to discuss the progress and problems that occurred during the week. He was referred to universally as 'NV' and addressed by employees as 'Mr V.'– he uses that acronym to this day.

Vinson used all available opportunities to instil the lesson that the interests of the customer are paramount. A brochure handed to each new employee on arrival stated:

> The company's growth has, to no small extent, depended on the fact that we have always made it a matter of supreme policy to give the best possible service to our customers who in the last count are, after all, the people who really employ us, as without them there would be no jobs.

In terms of employee relations, the company was highly advanced for a firm of its size, even judged by today's standards. It also became apparent that, when Vinson said all employees could expect to share in the company's success, he was serious. Rewards were given for ideas that increased productivity based on the scale of their impact, and a profit-sharing scheme based on monthly sales was introduced. There was a hard-luck fund for those who were encountering financial problems, free legal advice for those who needed it, and a pension scheme. Employees were encouraged to raise problems or grievances with the management, and a ten-year club and then a twenty-year club were created to reward long service. Employees were invited to bring friends and relatives to visit the factory to admire its progress, either by arrangement or on special 'Mums and Dads evenings'.

In addition, Vinson made a point of personally welcoming each new employee at the first available opportunity, a practice he continued even after the company expanded to four additional sites. Notes of congratulation were posted on the company's notice boards to give immediate recognition to those sections that had exceeded production or sales targets. Unusually for a manufacturing company at that time, the firm shared as much information with its employees as was practically possible, including details about profit margins and departmental productivity figures. An in-house newspaper entitled *Dippers' Digest*, featuring business, social and personal stories, was circulated to all employees; this was followed by the launch of *Crosslink*, a larger, glossier publication, with the aim of keeping employees up to date with developments at all of the company's factories as well as spreading important company messages. When employees were called to the phone to answer queries from customers, those giving the message over the public address system were asked to give the name of the caller and to convey as much information as possible in order to stress the link between the customer and those working on the production line, besides alerting those being summoned.

The firm also had an enlightened promotion scheme that enabled George Lawson, one of its first employees (who had started on the bench at £8 10s a week), to become sales manager at the company's Cheshire factory in the space of ten years.

Plastic Coatings's non-union status enabled the company to introduce innovations in working practices more quickly than might otherwise have been the case, and this fact, along with Vinson's enlightened employment policies, explains the total absence of industrial disputes during a period when Britain experienced its worst period of industrial relations.

Interviews with former employees confirm that Vinson's motivational skills were outstanding. 'He was charismatic and inspirational,' John Theobold, a former sales manager, recalls.

I respected, admired and revered him. I felt that if he said to me that he wanted me to go to France to sell, but I didn't have a ticket for the channel ferry, I would have plunged into the sea and swum there. Many years later I started my own business and owe its success to the inspirational business management I learned from him. Looking back I have no doubt he improved and enriched all of our lives.

Vinson's ability to motivate his staff and command their loyalty is borne out by statements of senior colleagues. Jeremy Peter-Hoblyn, a Cambridge graduate, was sufficiently impressed by Vinson and his company to leave a management job at GEC to join him at Plastic Coatings, where he increased efficiency and profits through the introduction of a rigorous system of financial controls.

Peter-Hoblyn, who had been introduced to Nigel by his London flatmate Mark Cannon Brookes, told me:

More than any other person I had worked with, he had the ability to make people feel that they were appreciated, that their role was important to the company's success, and that their suggestions would be taken seriously. He did this without trying to instil a false sense of their importance but with evident sincerity.

The firm's twin commitment to customers and employees was encapsulated in words displayed in the hall of its Guildford headquarters: 'In this company we not only cope, we care.'

Vinson's growing success, his reputation as an enlightened employer and his determination to recognise his responsibility to the community made him something of a local hero. The *Surrey Times and Advertiser* reported on 14 July 1970:

> There are some millionaires and self-made men, however, whose success no one resents. Guildford affords an example of a 'whizz-kid' of this kind – a man whose rapid rise to dramatic business success and personal fortune has evoked rather the reaction earned by a champion sportsman. Mr Nigel Vinson is the paradigm of the local boy made good. The place is proud of him and West Surrey people talk of his spectacular career with vicarious pleasure ... Plastics is, of course, a growth industry, and Nigel Vinson has helped it to grow and grown with it. To have done so in eighteen years without making more enemies than friends is a measure not only of his ability but also his personality. If heaven and hard work are destined to bestow such rewards on any man, nearly every one of his West

Surrey neighbours would agree that there is only one man in the area more richly deserving of them. There will be less agreement, however, over which other man.

Like all entrepreneurs, Vinson was not, of course, lacking in ego – a fact he later acknowledged:

> Apart from good health, entrepreneurs have to be egotistical. When you start up everybody thinks you must be mad or others would be having a go at the same thing. So you need an unproven self-confidence in your ability, and a blissful ignorance of the problems you are likely to encounter, allied to a determination to overcome every obstacle. Having started, you need essentially the ability of self-criticism, to learn from your mistakes, to kick your own backside, because nobody else will. Only those who have been successful in the world's eyes know how thin, in reality, the margin of success over failure is. Above all, success is seldom due to just one lucky choice, it is a compound of hundreds of little quarter per cents of attention to detail...

Despite the self-confessed sin of egotism, he was invariably at pains to stress the role of others in his success:

In business you need both the trade winds with you and the ability to be a frigate among the galleons – but it is not so much *what* you do as *how* you do it. All business is essentially a question of man management and sharing of problems ... I tried to run the company on common-sense lines, practising the simple belief of treating others as you would wish to be treated yourself, and following the age-old naval maxim of walking the ship – or being seen...

The ups and downs of business are both stimulating and worrying for the manager.

How do you tell a modern architect who insists on using your plastic coating to corrosion-proof the panels of the Dartford Tunnel – a job it would do perfectly – that he has overlooked the fact that if it caught alight it would give off noxious fumes and be highly dangerous – so sadly you must turn down his potentially huge contract that was otherwise just the business you badly needed?

The steady flow of sales lies at the heart of any successful business but, whatever the exhortations of government, small businesses should not attempt to export too early. The servicing and transport costs for export orders are huge and if something goes wrong it will be expensive to rectify. Exports are best done on the basis of a substantial home market where the product is fully tried and tested and after sales costs moderate. Rather than fly out to India to see potential customers, I suggested that they should come to see us and that we in turn would reimburse their hotel costs. They often jumped at the idea of having a holiday in the UK, to which they could bring their wives, and ultimately deals were completed at a fraction of the cost of going to them – and much goodwill established for the future.

Vinson was contemptuous of companies that enforced arbitrary distinctions between staff and workers by establishing separate canteens and entrances. He took great care to involve himself enthusiastically in the company's social events. An annual company dinner held at the Corona restaurant on Guildford high street – which became increasingly high-spirited as the company grew and prospered – began with Vinson brandishing a sword, with which he carved the roast meat. Such was the boisterousness of the occasion that, by prior arrangement, Nigel agreed to pay, should the restaurant dining room need to be redecorated after one event. John Theobold recalls that, after another such dinner, those present returned to the company's headquarters and Nigel could be seen on the roof directing a hose on the revellers below, who retaliated by taking aim with fire extinguishers. Company outings included a day trip on the Thames and a visit to the Goodwood races. The Christmas party followed a different theme each year, with presents for each of the children who attended.

When Plastic Coatings won the Queen's Award for industry in 1971, in recognition of its record of technical innovation, the ceremony – and the reception that followed – was attended not just by local dignitaries, board members and senior executives, but by employees from all five factories.

In many respects, Plastic Coatings had the feel of a family business, which is how several employees described it to me when I researched this book. Strictly speaking, it was no such thing: Vinson had created it from scratch rather than having inherited it and, until it was floated, he was the sole owner. But he was conscious that, if properly run, a business could satisfy the need to feel a sense of belonging, and this could best be achieved by enlightened employment policies as well as concern for the welfare of the staff. In turn, such feelings would foster bonds of loyalty to the company and a sense of unity. In these respects, the company did indeed display many of the characteristics of a well-run family firm.

There is no doubt that Vinson was motivated by a desire

to increase efficiency and maximise profits, but the moral flavour of many of his instructions to his senior staff make it clear that he believed that that was how a company CEO *ought* to behave and how a company *ought* to treat its staff. In a speech to the Durham Enterprise Club in 1992, he advised:

> Trust all people until you have cause not to. Don't automatically look for an ulterior motive or expect people to do you down. Trust is virtually always reciprocated and is the basis of all relationships. My maxim has always been to trust all people until you have cause not to. One must enter into all relationships on this basis. However, experience has taught me that the Russian *dovorey no provorey* – trust but verify – has much merit. The person you trust is safe-guarded by the verification of audit, both from the malfeasance of others (for which they might have got the blame) and from temptation (which unverified pickings might have made irresistible). No honest person resents an audit – though I did think, and still do, that in a sense it is an insult to their integrity.

He also urged senior colleagues to own up if they realised that they had criticised subordinates unfairly. And it is clear that, while he expected his sales staff to strike hard bargains with suppliers and customers, he counselled against seeking too hard a bargain: 'Leave something in it for the other guy – don't strike too hard a bargain, and one day you may be grateful that he hasn't forgotten your fairness.'

For Vinson, it was a happy coincidence that doing the right thing ethically so often proved to be the right thing in terms of long-term business success – an insight that would not have surprised Adam Smith, but would not necessarily meet with the approval of some contemporary advocates of unbridled free-market economies.

Vinson strongly believed that the kind of corporate culture he had successfully created at Plastic Coatings would be jeopardised if work units grew too large; in his view, small was indeed beautiful. He later explained: 'We used a comb structure, each part independent but held together by a strong central spine of services.' Vinson, who memorably described takeovers as 'megalomania masquerading as efficiency', later reflected on the importance of restricting the size of work units:

> People want to relate to their activity. Units should be sized, where possible, so that people feel that they are treated as names, not numbers, and know that their contribution can be seen to count.

Apart from the more obvious justifications for small businesses – economic vitality, dispersed initiative, disseminated economic power, sources of invention, etc. – there is one equally, if not more, important justification: man's need to belong.

Vinson had read and admired *Small Is Beautiful: A Study of Economics As If People Mattered* by E. F. Schumacher. The title of Schumacher's highly influential book of essays is somewhat misleading, since it does not argue that smallness is a virtue in itself. However, it did rail very effectively against the then fashionable presumption that big was automatically better – a realisation Vinson had reached by himself. Vinson was subsequently introduced to Schumacher by the latter's son Christian, whose own work on industrial organisation Vinson was later to encourage and generously support.

Despite his belief that work units should remain small, and his conviction that the value of Britain's small enterprises to the national economy was greatly underestimated, Vinson's own company was growing rapidly. Turnover had increased every year since it had been founded, rising from £121,000 in 1959 to £1.6 million in 1968 (£24 million in today's money), with pre-tax profits rising from £16,958 in 1959 to £161,788 (£2.4 million in present-day values).

The company, which had become the largest and most

technologically advanced company of its kind in the world, was floated by tender in January 1969 with a minimum price set at 15 shillings a share, at a price/earnings ratio of twenty to four. The shares were massively oversubscribed.

Vinson gave 10 per cent of the shares to directors and employees, according to a formula that took into account seniority and length of service.

Although he remained chairman and CEO of the company following the flotation, it is likely that he was beginning to think of new challenges. It is therefore probable that his motive in rewarding his workforce in this way was simply what he said it was – to acknowledge their loyalty – rather than a means to encourage an already loyal and incentivised staff.

'I wanted to say thank you for all that they had done for me,' he later explained. Vinson, a man of strong feelings as well as strong convictions, recalled how moved he had been when one of his employees approached him to say: 'Guv, you don't know what it means to feel that I own a bit of the company.'

The mechanics of the flotation were handled by Nigel's friend Mark Cannon Brookes, with whom he shared a London house and who was then employed by the City brokerage firm of L. Messel. Cannon Brookes recalls that the broad outlines of the float were decided by Vinson himself:

There is no doubt that the float could have been organised in a way which would have enabled Nigel to have walked away with far more in his back pocket than he did. But by shrewdly opting for a sale by tender at a sensible price Nigel impressed the City and ensured that the share price steadily rose. What was remarkable to many people was that every employee – including the man who swept the floor – profited from the sale. Perhaps, it is a pity that his example has not been more widely followed.

In 1971, the year that Plastic Coatings received the Queen's Award for industry, Imperial Tobacco bought the company for £4.7 million, including Vinson's 54 per cent holding. 'Imps' had first approached him three years earlier. He considered it to be the best long-term partner because of its intention to run the company as an autonomous unit – and its excellent pension fund. For those reasons, he chose to accept the offer rather than face the possibility that an unsuitable offer might come in the future at a time when he no longer had a controlling interest.

Mark Cannon Brookes believes that, in addition to wanting to diversify away from tobacco, one reason for Imperial's bid was its desire to capture the services of a young and dynamic business leader. But Nigel, a lifelong non-smoker, turned down an offer to join the Imperial Board and, by agreement, gave up the post of Plastic Coatings chairman the following year to become its non-executive chairman.

> Everything went as we had agreed at the outset and was done on the basis of trust. There were no contracts. At the end of two years as non-executive chairman I asked Imperial: 'Are you happy? Is the management succession working out? Staff relations all right?' All of this was fine, so we shook hands and parted amicably.

A number of Vinson's contemporaries were surprised by his decision to sell. Apart from his desire to develop a wider range of interests and play a part in public life, he may have feared that the company's continuing rapid growth would mean he would no longer be able to have a hands-on role. He enjoyed the close intimacy with his employees, which he had come to take for granted, and the next stage of the company's growth would therefore not be as reward-ing or fulfilling.

He also doubted the value of simply pursuing a path of personal enrichment. 'What's the point? You can only eat three meals a day.' And he clearly sensed that his freedom of action was slipping away.

> As chairman of a public company you have power and prestige, but you are not a free man. The require- ment for quarterly reporting, which I think was a great mistake, narrowed time horizons and discouraged intelligent long-term planning. And, of course, busi- ness is no longer fun when you can't walk the ship.

Sixty years on, the company is still doing extremely well and is a leader in its field worldwide, thus vindicating Vinson's choice of business: corrosion- or rust-proofing is always needed.

After the successful flotation of his company, Vinson was in great demand as a non-executive director. His close friend Michael Stoddart, head of Electra Investment Trust (a lead- ing venture capital fund), was one of the first to engage his services. Enjoying the task and contributing practical advice – as he did elsewhere in the City – based on a fairly unique background of business development, he remained on the board for twenty years, the last ten as deputy chairman. Sub- sequently, at Michael's retirement party, Nigel finished his peon of praise: 'Come on, Mike – for the last of your deals, how about a bid for meals on wheels!'

CHAPTER 3

In search of a wife

NIGEL'S EARLY YEARS as a fast-rising entrepreneur left little time for a social life. But,
as success came, he found opportunities to
ride, fish and entertain, and not least to find
a wife.

His home in those years was a first-floor flat in the Old
Rectory, a beautiful but run-down eighteenth-century
vicarage at Upton Grey in Hampshire, part of which
Nigel and his mother initially rented from the Church

commissioners. When the Church decided to build a new vicarage he bought the old one, along with half an acre of gardens and a paddock in which he would keep his horse. He then set about lovingly restoring and modernising the house, which was to be his home for ten years. His mother, who took an obvious pride in his growing success and who missed no opportunity to encourage him to find the right girl to marry, moved to a cottage a short distance away 'to make him get on with it'. Sadly, she died there before he did so.

Hunting became a regular weekend event to which he increasingly looked forward, enjoying the social opportunities that membership of the Hampshire Hunt provided, as well as the challenge and excitement of the chase. He made many lifelong friends over this period.

As secretary of the organising committee, he ran the Hunt Ball for four years in succession with typical enthusiasm and brio, engaging the services not only of a dance band, quintet and a DJ for the 1971 event, but also nightclub acts and a palm reader called Madam Zara.

Visits to London for business or pleasure were made more congenial when he came to share a rented flat in South Kensington with a friend, Michael Jodrell. They had met, quite by chance, as the result of a painting.

Nigel's mother had an outstanding eye for form and

beauty, which Nigel, to some degree, inherited. Passing through Shere in Surrey in 1959 she saw, in the window of an antiques dealer, a painting that, because of the colours and style, she felt certain must be a Munnings – but it was unsigned. Trusting her judgement, she bought it for £40. Nigel subsequently took the painting – a landscape of chestnut trees in flower – to Agnew's to see whether it could be authenticated. 'I believe this might be a Munnings,' he said somewhat diffidently to the dealer.

'Of course it's a Munnings,' came the blunt reply.

'But it is unsigned,' said Nigel.

'It won't be for long,' said the dealer. 'He is coming in tomorrow and I will get him to sign it for you.'

Two days later, Nigel collected the picture en route to a drinks party and, as he was taking it out of the taxi, a man of about the same years as himself approached and said, 'Can I help? I expect you are going to the same party … Do tell me about the picture you have got there.' Michael Jodrell and Nigel became lifelong friends.

One evening, Nigel introduced Michael to a Hampshire acquaintance, Veronica Boord, little realising that the introduction would put an end to what had been an ideal flat-sharing arrangement. Michael subsequently proposed and married Veronica, whereupon Nigel moved out to share with Mark Cannon Brookes – another stockbroker friend who was later to act on his behalf when Plastic Coatings was floated on the London Stock Exchange.

When the lease on their flat expired, Nigel suggested they jointly purchase a house. Cannon Brookes explained that he had no money and therefore could not stump up his half of the deposit, but Nigel came up with a solution: he would use his share of the property as security in order to enable his friend to obtain the mortgage.

Cannon Brookes recalls:

> The arrangement was typically Nigel: imaginative, but practical. Although we agreed that everything should be done on a fifty/fifty basis the deal was far more advantageous to me since I was starting on the property ladder without having any capital at all, while Nigel was already doing well and could have obviously bought somewhere wholly on his own account. We found a three-bedroomed house in Crescent Place off the Brompton Road which was ideally suited to our bachelor needs. We had different interests – unlike Nigel I am completely apolitical – but we got on terribly well, and we have remained good friends ever since.
>
> Nigel would arrive from Guildford in his Aston Martin, breeze in full of enthusiasm about what he

was currently up to and then disappear to see other friends or to take a girl out to dinner. I might then see him the following morning over breakfast for half an hour before he returned to Guildford. Although generous, he disliked waste or extravagance and I remember him once querying the milkman's bill. But he made absolutely no complaint about paying half the whisky bill, when I was responsible for at least nine-tenths of the consumption!

At the time we were both looking for wives and we agreed from the outset that whoever married first would buy the other out, which is what in the event happened when I married in 1961. Later, when my wife and I moved to a larger family house I sold at a considerable profit.

At weekends, I frequently stayed at his house in Upton Grey, which at that time belonged partly to his vicar. There were some tremendous weekend parties – well described as 'a bit of a marriage market' – which led the vicar to comment that as much as he loved Nigel, he had always believed hell was underground and now realised this was not the case at weekends. The vicar's weekend ordeal came to an end when Nigel bought out the vicar's half of the house on generous terms.

In fact, the parties are likely to have been less riotous than the vicar's remarks suggest: they were usually held over lunch rather than dinner – a preference that reflected Nigel's dislike of late nights and his lifelong habit of getting a good night's sleep in order to rise early – and they were sometimes attended by the vicar, who became a good friend. Nigel remained unmarried.

Vinson's friendship with Cannon Brookes was to prove long-lasting. On the occasion of his friend's sixty-fifth birthday, Nigel composed the following lines:

Happy Birthday Dear Marko

How on earth did you achieve it?
My God, I can't believe it!
You're sixty-five today!
Fifteen till you're eighty
So come on my old matey
Don't leave it till you're grey!
Now is the time to blew it
Don't even think you'll rue it.
Yes, now's the time to do it.
Now is the time for play.
Soon comes the adult nappy
So come on, make it snappy.

Come on you gorgeous Pappy
Get out and make your hay!

Although highly eligible, and increasingly keen to marry and raise a family, Nigel found the search for a wife more difficult than many of his friends did, something that caused him considerable heart-searching.

On returning from national service to live at Nettle-stead, Nigel had enjoyed a brief but passionate affair with a local girl called Amanda, but quickly realised they were probably unsuited. However, the parameters of that experience went deep and made it hard for him to find a comparable relationship.

On the face of it, Nigel was the answer to every mother's dream for her daughter: rich, successful, good-looking, charming, generous, well-dressed, good-natured, sincere and possessing a love of children as well as of paintings and expensive motor cars. In practice, Nigel was not as successful in the pursuit of a dream spouse as he had hoped, and, although ultimately very successful indeed, the search took years longer than he anticipated.

The seriousness with which he pursued the ideal wife, combined with being a bit of a perfectionist, seems to have worked against him. It didn't help that, as a result of being reared in an all-male household and at all-male schools, he was shy in female company. Peter Bedford, a longstanding friend – who later arranged the insurance on his business and on his Northumberland farms and subsequently enabled him to become a Lloyds name – remembers Nigel's frustration at not being able to find the right girl:

> Although more successful in his career than most of his contemporaries he was not as successful with girls as he would have liked. He was so keen to make himself agreeable he could sometimes appear awkward or gauche. Also some girls may have realised that because of his remarkable energy and dominant personality he would not have been easy to live with. And then, of course there is his taste in puns…
>
> In the event, the long wait was worthwhile … Vonnie was the perfect match: a hugely sympathetic and calming influence: attractive, sensible and loving.

'Vonnie' is Yvonne Collin – a speech therapist and, like Nigel's mother, a doctor's daughter – whom he married at the age of forty-one.

He had proposed to Vonnie, who is nine years younger than him, over a kissing gate at Upton Grey on 29 May – her birthday. As his father was unwell, they had decided to move quickly, obtaining a special licence and marrying within the fortnight. As Nigel put it: 'It was ten days between the "Will you?" and the "I will".'

He had met her six years earlier at a lunch party. Both had been in other relationships at the time, and, although he followed up the meeting with a gift of red roses (a gesture that raised eyebrows at the Queen Elizabeth hospital in Hackney, where Vonnie was working), the relationship did not blossom. Nevertheless, Vonnie made a sufficient impression on Nigel – who has written occasional poetry throughout his life, some romantic, some humorous – to inspire him to compose the following lines, which he later sent to her:

Enigma: To Yvonne

If love's the union of two minds
How does one find a mind of similar kind?
If love's the union of two hearts
How does one find a heart of matching part?
Perhaps the one great lesson that life shows
Is that love that really matters grows and grows.
Love based on pity is a flickering flame
Love based on passion flares up to die again.
In love without real love one-sided consummation is but pain.

But love is totality of body, mind and eyes
This is the love that ever growing never dies.
And so my greatest wish for you dear Yvonne
Is that you find such happiness anon.

Vonnie's first impression of Nigel was of 'someone very energetic, quick-witted, sensitive and very aware [of others] who was also a little bit of a smart Alec. I had always gone in for lame ducks, and Nigel is precisely the opposite of that. So I quickly decided that he wasn't my type at all.'

Vonnie's brother Professor Richard Collin, an eye surgeon, became a firm friend of Nigel – who subsequently quipped: 'Marry one and get one free!'

But Yvonne was not the first girl to whom he had proposed – he had broken off a previous engagement ten days before the wedding ceremony was due to take place. He later told friends:

> It was by far the most painful thing I have ever had to do. I hated the idea of hurting her, but I became convinced that the marriage would end in unhappiness and divorce and that I would hurt her still more if the marriage went ahead. I had to summon all my reserves of courage – it was the toughest decision of my life.

A close friend Peter Bedford remembers being deeply moved by Nigel's predicament:

> He was hugely upset, but I am quite sure that if he had not taken the decision that he did, there would have been even greater unhappiness. His mistake was to propose the marriage, which happened, I suspect, because of his strong desire to raise a family and his growing frustration at not being able to find the right girl.

Nigel said later:

> In life if you believe something to be wrong, even though it is your own fault, then it must be better to admit that belief and to face the situation truthfully, rather than make a compromise ... One's desire to get married is not reason enough for marrying somebody, if you really care for their happiness.

Following his decision to call off the wedding, he had the painful task of writing to 200 wedding guests, returning gifts that had already been received and cancelling the reception that was to have followed at the bride's home. He also had the job of writing to a wider group of friends and neighbours who had been invited to a lunch at Upton Grey the following month to meet his bride. A simple letter to those invited read: 'We have decided not to go ahead, and you will know that this difficult decision was not taken lightly. I am doubly sorry to disappoint friends like yourself, who were so anxious to see one happily married.'

This was an empty and poignant period in his life, as this short verse reveals:

The small things in life that please
A smile, a thought, shared interests – these
Are values giving peace not stress –
As found in the touch of your caress.
Now passing your picture on the wall
Yes, these are the memories I recall.

His subsequent marriage to Vonnie brought emotional stability, companionship and love. They started to go out with each other five years after their initial introduction. When they met again at a dinner party, Nigel asked Vonnie whether she would date him if he invited her. Vonnie replied that she might. When he called a few days later, she pleaded that the pressure of work, and the MSc for which she was studying in the few hours the hospital regime allowed, made this difficult. But Nigel was characteristically persistent and she gave in.

> When later Nigel asked me to marry him I thought:
> now this is going to be challenging … A close friend,
> who encouraged the relationship, told me that I would
> be good for him and he would be good for me, which
> I think has turned out to be true.

The marriage took place on 10 June 1972 at Nettlestead Church and was followed by a wedding breakfast in the crypt at Nettlestead Place for the couple, the bride's parents, Nigel's father and thirty close friends – to whom Nigel quipped in typical style: 'It's on with the shackles and out with the shekels!'

Yvonne turned out to be the most loving wife and mother, a very good cook and a huge support to him. She ran their large home and a bevy of helpers who, like her breed of dogs – 'Roddams' (half Flatcoat, half Labrador) – were devoted to her.

As he later said, after a long wait 'at last he had found "Miss Right" and not "Miss Nearly-Wright"'!

CHAPTER 4

Emancipating the workers

A S A YOUNG man working as a salesman for Creators – the plastics company that gave Vinson his only experience as an employee – he encountered, for the first time, the class barriers that he quickly concluded discouraged social mobility and impeded industrial efficiency in Britain at the time – and perhaps, to an extent, still do. The fact that many such barriers have disappeared, or become less rigid than formerly, owes much to the influence of people like Marks & Spencer boss Marcus Sieff, Nigel Vinson and other business leaders, many of whom are associated with the Industrial Participation Association (IPA), which Vinson chaired from 1971 to 1978.

Vinson later recalled the experience that led him to realise how much would have to change if Britain were to reverse its relative economic decline: 'I remember going into one factory, and as we walked along the corridor, I saw this notice – "No workers beyond this point". I could feel my hackles rise in repugnance against such a statement.'

Although he was only twenty years old at the time, it was at this moment he became aware of the fact that many of Britain's industrial problems were self-inflicted through the perpetuation of social barriers and the confusion of class and status. 'We confuse two things in industry – status and class,' he told a meeting of the Industrial Co-Partnership Association, the forerunner of the IPA, in July 1967.

The association existed to promote 'a sense of common purpose at work', but it is striking that when Vinson was asked to address the meeting at Girton College, Cambridge, its seventeen-man executive committee included only one trade unionist. Its list of vice-presidents included two viscounts, a marquis and several knights of the realm, as well as a few retired senior military officers. The shop floor was also under-represented in the list of speakers, even though time was found in the programme for the chairman's wife to describe a recent visit to the Holy Land, complete with colour slides.

He told those present:

> It is still common in industry today to give office work-ers 'staff status' and to regard them as inherently superior beings from a social, moral and capability point of view to those on the shop floor.
>
> This is mumbo-jumbo of the first order, and is mix-ing status and class. If, at Waterloo station, all quite happily use the same lavatories, why on earth can't everyone use the same lavatories in a factory? Encour-aging artificial social barriers of this type promotes an attitude of 'we' and 'they' and is fundamentally bad for the philosophy of a company.

His audience was probably more ready than many of Brit-ain's industrial leaders to contemplate the removal of social barriers, perceived by very few at that time to stand in the way of economic progress. To most people, Vinson's arguments in favour of emancipating those engaged in manufacturing from their status as 'workers', and conse-quently as inferior social beings, would have come across as radical.

Vinson, who on other occasions condemned separate canteens and entrances for staff and workers, went on to explain how he tried to bridge the gap between the two at Plastic Coatings:

> As part of a concerted policy to encourage personal responsibilities, we are trying to move to the old conception of staff status – but for everybody. The word 'staff' has come to lose its meaning in industrial terms, and now rather than describe everybody who works for an organisation, it's definitely associated with 'they'. It's very much of the management and workers' philosophy. Thus we have dropped the use of the term and prefer, when talking about different categories, to use the word grades. In our attempts to eliminate the exclusivity of the staff grade, and to close the gap between 'them' and the factory workers, we have not attempted to pick up the shop floor personnel and lift them across the chasm that previously existed. What we are trying to do is to fill the chasm with concrete [measures], so that progressive steps can be taken to cross the gap.

Vinson was not, of course, arguing the case for social egalitarianism, but for a form of meritocracy that had no room for

class distinctions although fully recognised the importance
of status. As he explained, this meant not only giving fore-
men and junior managers the keys to the factories in which
they worked – and making sure their pay, privileges and
holiday entitlements were superior to those beneath them
– but also giving them as much responsibility as possible,
including the right to hire and fire. They were also given
the authority to give employees the day off if they believed
there to be an overriding personal case for doing so.

> Every now and again the odd privileges we give are
> abused – but this to my way of thinking is no reason to
> stop giving them. For every occasion one is kicked in
> the teeth for doing a good deed, there are ninety-nine
> other moments when it is recognised, appreciated,
> remembered. Because somebody abuses a privilege
> there is no reason why everybody else should be
> penalised.

Vinson went on to make a passionate case for better communication and for humanising industrial relations,
explaining how, at his own factories, the names of those
who were celebrating a birthday, or the anniversary of their
start date at the company, were circulated to all heads of
department: 'Then when the departmental head goes

round, he can say "Good morning, Fred – happy birthday," or, "Good morning, George – I can't see how you have stuck working in this firm for ten years, you must be crazy!"'

However, department heads were subsequently advised to modify the approach when it was discovered that not all female employees welcomed news of their birthdays being broadcast by their bosses.

Although at the time Vinson's approach to industrial relations was regarded as unconventional, his words found favour with Sir Geoffrey Shakespeare, the Industrial co-Partnership's chairman, who subsequently wrote to congratulate him on his 'splendid address':

> It was exactly the kind of talk that we need so much and rarely get. I mean it. The story of one who builds up his business, finds difficulties for himself, all the mistakes to avoid and the variety of all the little things that make all the difference to good management. It was a fascinating talk, and if I may say so, you delivered it with great charm and conviction.

At the conference, Vinson found common cause and developed a friendship with his Guildford neighbour James More-Molyneux, the proprietor of the well-regarded Loseley Park Ice Cream and Loseley Building Products. Ten years later, Nigel offered James's son Mike a studentship on his Hetton Estate in Northumberland. Subsequently, Mike was introduced to, and fell in love with, a local girl called Sarah Westmacott – 'a different form of co-partnership', as Nigel was heard to say at their wedding.

Today the IPA, which is funded by membership subscriptions and fees from consultancy and training services, continues in its task of helping managers and employees to develop new ways of working, based on trust and collaboration.

Vinson was also a leading member of the Working Together Campaign, whose purpose was to create a greater sense of mutual interest among management and workers.

In a pamphlet published as part of the campaign, Vinson argued that the importance of good human relations in industry was constantly in danger of being overlooked since such factors could not easily be measured, and because of the tendency towards large-scale units.

> What we must do is to transplant the regard for the best family businesses across to the bigger company. Managers must be given the maximum autonomy to be the 'gaffer' on the ground, to be the man to whom people can turn and know they will get a square deal and a square answer.

> How much of the social and industrial unrest today
> is due to the fact that people now have the money
> and education to know that they should be treated
> as somebody, and yet are still treated as nobodies? In
> the rush for growth through bigness we have gone for
> wealth and forgotten self-respect – it must be possible
> to aim for both.

Vinson went on to offer a 'names not numbers' approach to industrial relations based on human decency, common sense and shrewd insights into the country's prevailing problems.

Industrialists were advised to drop the practice of having separate entrances and to introduce universal staff status, while taking care not to erode differentials that recognised skills and status. Nigel suggested that rises and rockets be delivered privately with due sense of occasion rather than publicly on the shop floor. So he urged companies to provide sound-proofed offices, enabling staff to talk quietly and in private when necessary.

Based on his experience at Plastic Coatings, he went on to encourage the introduction of share incentive schemes, profit sharing, hard-luck funds, open evenings and a host of small practical measures such as remembering to look people in the eye and sharing information widely in order

to improve communications and reduce areas of mis-
understanding or suspicion. As described earlier, those
giving messages about orders over the PA system were
encouraged to provide detailed information about the
callers in order to remind employees of the importance
of the customer:

> Not only does being nice to your neighbour make the
> world a much more pleasant place, but it fosters a sense
> of goodwill and the knowledge that management cares
> and is seen to care, making a much more satisfactory and
> profitable business; and that it is right for everybody
> who works in it and for the nation as a whole.

Today, some of Vinson's advice might appear obvious or trite,
but in the industrial environment of the 1970s – brilliantly
portrayed in the '50s Boulting Brothers' film *I'm All Right
Jack* – it would have made uncomfortable reading for those
who believed that their background or class absolved them
from the need to change established ways of doing things.
It is also possible to discern tensions and contradictions in
the Vinson proposals for transforming Britain's industrial
relations. This is apparent from two articles: one written by
him in the *Daily Telegraph* on 19 December 1977, advocat-
ing handing over the ownership of the coal mines to the

miners and the creation of self-supporting workers' coop-eratives; another written by a business journalist describing Nigel's achievements at Plastic Coatings.

The first of these, headed 'Let the workers think for themselves' – in which he argued in favour of granting individuals greater freedom and responsibility and, where possible, a share of the ownership – was typical of his other articles and speeches.

But the article about his achievements at Plastic Coatings – which stressed the central duty of bosses and managers to 'care' for those who worked for them – appeared in the magazine *Business Administration* in 1973 and was headed: 'What the hell's wrong with good paternalism?'

Vinson is enough of a libertarian to want employees to have greater freedom and independence, but he also believes that employers should genuinely care about the welfare of those who work for them; if there is a contradiction between these two attitudes it is not one that worries him.

As Britain moved from a paternalistic to a market-based society, such contradictions were perhaps inevitable. 'Care' is a favourite Vinson word, which marks him out from many of those who helped lay the foundations of Thatcherism. The truth is that, while hating the notion of state paternal-ism, Vinson believes that bosses should show kindness and generosity to those under them, and not merely because in the long run it pays off – although he is confident that, in most circumstances, it does (hence his decisions to reward the employees of Plastic Coatings with a share of the proceeds when the company was sold and buy a house for his long-serving secretary as thanks for her loyalty and hard work).

Although from an affluent, and in some ways privileged, background, Vinson is a self-made man. But he is not the kind of meritocrat who discounts the role of luck or believes his success is entirely due to his own merits – a belief that, as one observer has noted, can lead to an attitude of 'I earned it, I deserve it; I owe it to no one, thank nobody'.[2]

Vinson believes that his good fortune in life confers a moral obligation to help others. When I was researching this book, he drew my attention to the following passage from Luke 12:48: 'From everyone to whom much has been given, much will be required; and from the one to whom much has been entrusted, even more will be required'.

In his view, one's obligations go beyond the merely legal and formal.

His thinking was also influenced by reading *The Life of Robert Owen* – one of his mother's heroes.

---

2 Ed Smith, 'A bastardised understanding of meritocracy has become part of bling self-indulgence', *New Statesman*, 14–20 June 2013.

The desire to promote measures and work practices that enhance job satisfaction and give employees a greater sense of self-esteem is reflected in an undated brief Nigel prepared for the purpose of speech making, which includes the following items of advice:

> *Employees work with you, not for you*
> *Machines should work for people, not people for machines*
> *Why should war give a sense of unity?*
> *The present system frustrates a worker's natural desire to participate*
> *The British people are the nation's greatest asset.*

Throughout his life, Vinson has been at pains to stress the importance of trust.

His friend and neighbour, the author and journalist Matt Ridley – who, as Viscount Ridley, sits alongside him on the Tory benches in the House of Lords – told the author:

> There is one thing that he said many years ago in a lecture that has stayed with me and proved very much right in my experience. The lecture was on entrepreneurship and he said that one key rule was 'trust people unless you have a reason not to'. This struck me as generous, open and yet sensible. I see many

people failing to open opportunities to work with others by failing to offer trust. Game theory vindicates Nigel's approach by showing that the most profitable strategy in an iterated prisoner's dilemma game is to cooperate in the first round and then to do whatever your opponent did in the previous round – to offer cooperation but be prepared to punish defection with defection. I think it is characteristically astute of Nigel to have put it in words better than anybody I know.

The dehumanising effect of large-scale industrial organisations in which individuals are given little idea of how their work related to other aspects of the industrial process has also been a major source of reflection and concern.

His subsequent experience as a board member of major companies such as the British Airports Authority (1973–80) and Barclays Bank (1982–88) confirmed his belief that the benefits of scale were often exaggerated, that large companies should be composed of manageable units and that decisions should be decentralised in order to avoid the dehumanising consequences of size. 'Size is the curse of our time. The larger the unit, the more the serfs, the fewer the freemen,' he wrote in a collection of sayings, published upon his retirement.

At a meeting of the IPA in Cambridge, Vinson – who

had been very impressed by the book *Small is Beautiful* – listened with fascination to a young executive from British Steel called Christian Schumacher – son of the book's author – who argued that many prevailing economic and industrial problems were a result of the fragmentation of society and man's alienation from God. Society could recover and prosper if ways could be found to integrate the main tenets of the Christian faith into the organisation and structure of the modern workplace. Schumacher offered practical examples of how this might be done and gave instances of where this had increased efficiency.

At the conclusion of Schumacher's talk, Vinson asked to join him on a walk through Cambridge so that he could learn more about his views. During their stroll, Schumacher explained that he hoped to enlarge upon these in a book, but that – because of the long hours he put in as a junior executive at British Steel and the responsibilities of bringing up a young family – he was making poor progress. 'Would it help if you could afford to employ a secretary?' Vinson asked. When Schumacher said that it would, Vinson produced a cheque book as they walked and wrote out a cheque for £2,000 – equivalent to £20,000 in 2014 values.

The result was *To Live and Work: A Theological Interpretation*, published seven years later – during which time Vinson continued to offer encouragement, suggestions and friendship.

In the preface to the book, Schumacher wrote, 'I am particularly grateful to Nigel Vinson whose practical generosity, advice and friendship enabled me to write anything at all'; and in the foreword to the book, Vinson wrote that in 'an increasingly anonymous and rootless world' Schumacher had given 'hope for a future in which people can both live and work in balance and find fulfilment in doing so.'

Schumacher's book led to a fellowship at the LSE and subsequently to the creation of Work Structuring Limited, which he set up with the help of his wife Diana. The company advised other companies on organisational redesign in order to improve their performances, and it was based on Schumacher's concept of 'whole work'. To be 'whole', a workgroup had to bear the characteristics of being 'a body', of being mystical and of being 'of Christ' – 'just like the church'. In other words, Schumacher used the concept of the Holy Trinity to produce a blueprint for relationships in the workplace. Major companies were more interested in Schumacher's claims of being able to improve productivity and profits than in Christian theology, but a growing number took his ideas seriously and introduced changes to their organisational structures as a result. These have included Corus, Exxon, GlaxoSmithKline, ICI, General Electric, Lever Bros, Monsanto, Phillips Electronics, Pilkington, Reckitt & Colman,

Shell, Texaco and Unilever, as well as companies in South Africa, Australia and New Zealand. Schumacher also redesigned the organisational structure of Chester Zoo; it is not known what the impact was on the animals, but the introduction of his ideas was followed by an immediate 25 per cent increase in the number of visitors.

A simple list of clients probably understates the extent of Schumacher's influence, since a number of those employed by the mentioned companies are known to have subsequently applied his ideas when moving to other firms.

Schumacher believes that his meeting with Vinson was one of the foundations of his subsequent success. When I met him in March 2013 he told me: 'If Nigel hadn't encouraged me and provided practical support and friendship, my life might have taken a very different course and I might not have enjoyed whatever influence I have had. Our meeting represented a turning point in my life.'

Although a church warden at St Michael's & All Angels in Ilderton, Nigel's religious views are of a different order to those of Schumacher – whose work depends as much on biblical texts as on empirical research. While accepting the Christian ethic and believing that fulfilment can only be achieved through engagement with others, Vinson does not believe in a literal interpretation of the Bible.

His memory of their first conversations has faded, but it

seems unlikely that Nigel accepted uncritically everything that Schumacher, a Christian visionary, had to say. But, as in many other instances, his help was immediate and unconditional. It was given because he took an instant liking to Schumacher and was impressed by his evident goodness and sincerity. He also judged – correctly as things turned out – that his new friend's ideas had the potential to do something to humanise the workplace and give individuals much greater satisfaction from their working lives.

As chairman of the Industrial Participation Association, Vinson spoke extensively on industrial relations and companies' organisational structures, and he was selected by Lord Watkinson to become a member of his committee looking into 'the responsibility of the British public company'. This led to him being asked to speak on Business Ethics at a weekend seminar for industrialists, held at St George's, Windsor Castle – and known colloquially as the Duke of Edinburgh's think tank.

He got on well with Kenneth Adams, the director of St George's, who asked him to assist with promoting Industry Year – believing that Britain is 'an industrial nation with an anti-industrial culture' and that this should be reversed. Campaigning took place with business leaders throughout the country, many of whom were encouraged by Vinson, but the project was not helped when, on a visit to see Norman Lamont, the then Minister for Industry, they were told in as many words that they were wasting their time and no government funds would be available.

Subsequently Vinson was asked to become a trustee of St George's, which he did for five years – helping to develop their industry programmes – before then declining the post of assistant treasurer, as getting to Windsor Castle by 10 a.m. on a Monday for meetings chaired by the Duke of Edinburgh meant leaving Northumberland on a Sunday and spoiling a precious weekend with the family.

CHAPTER 5

Changing the political weather and serving the Queen

WHILE PLASTIC COATINGS was booming, the British economy was entering a period of relatively rapid economic decline. Nigel Vinson had come to share the views of those commentators who feared the economy might be on the brink of absolute decline, although profits and growth in his own company had increased every year since its launch and employee relations were excellent: there had not been a single significant industrial dispute. Meanwhile, labour relations in the UK were among the worst in the industrialised world, with strikes accounting for an average of 12.9 million lost days of work in the '70s and peaking at more than 29 million days in 1979. Having started his own company with modest capital and without business or technical training of any kind, he reflected on why it was that Britain should be crippled by industrial stoppages and lamentable productivity if his own employees enjoyed turning up for work in the morning and their order books were consistently full. If he could succeed from such modest beginnings, why couldn't others?

Throughout his life, Vinson has sought to persuade Britain's business directors that it's in their own interests to ensure their employees are treated with respect and that working conditions allow them to derive maximum satisfaction from their tasks. He had strong ideas how this might be accomplished and began to reflect more widely on the measures necessary to rescue the country from, what was increasingly referred to as, the 'British disease'. He began to advance these ideas in articles, as well as business and political forums, with the confidence expected of a young, highly energetic and successful entrepreneur. Vinson had already concluded that state ownership of industry was a disaster and he frequently repeated a phrase that, in his view, went right to the heart of the problem: 'Where nobody really owns, nobody really cares' – a saying originally attributed to Aristotle.

He also doubted whether the state had the necessary skills to intervene directly in the economy and prop up failing companies, or the ability to guarantee full employment. He had, in short, grasped that the uncoordinated wisdom of the market was superior to centralised economic planning and, while not perfect, capitalism was superior to alternative economic systems. He wanted business organisations and the Tory leadership to be more robust in capitalism's defence; he believed they should claim the moral high ground by stressing the link between market order and liberty.

Unlike some of those who were to play a role in the Thatcher revolution, he did not regard free-market economics as a secular religion and he realised that markets function best in societies based on strong moral foundations.

Extensive reading does not appear to have played a key role in the development of his thinking, although he did read the *Financial Times* from the age of seventeen and had been head librarian at Pangbourne. However, two books plainly made a mark. The first was *Atlas Shrugged* – Ayn Rand's dystopian novel about what happens when the risk-taking and wealth-creating abilities of the entrepreneur are stifled by the state. He read this while enjoying his own early success as an entrepreneur: '*Atlas Shrugged* by Ayn Rand has moved many people and not least me. Her description of building up and creating a business – the joy of creation through the manufacture of useful things – went right to my heart.' The second book was Frederich von Hayek's *The Road to Serfdom*, in which the Austrian economist and philosopher warned of the tyranny that results from systems of centralised economic planning. Later, Vinson was to do all he could to ensure that this latter work was made available as a low-cost student edition.

His first contributions to public debate in the 1960s were based on his experience as an entrepreneur, but these ideas were refined as a result of reflection and increasing contact with economists and policy analysts. At the time, however, such views did not command majority support. The boardrooms of Britain's top companies and Britain's political and intellectual elite were either hostile to Vinson's contributions, or believed that the prevailing climate of ideas and opinion made their introduction impractical. From the start, Vinson was critical of the Confederation of British Industry (CBI), its corporatist tendencies and its acceptance of conventional economic wisdom, but he joined its Small Firms Council and subsequently became its deputy chairman; he was then invited by John Methuen to join the influential president's committee.

Nigel also started the Young Enterprise organisation's Guildford branch, became chairman of his local Young Conservatives, joined the Bow Group (whose members at that time included several future ministers such as Geoffrey Howe, Norman Lamont, Leon Brittan and Peter Lilley), and wrote for its magazine *Crossbow*.

He even thought about becoming an MP, but after one failed attempt in Aldershot in 1974 – where his bachelor status clearly worked against him – he abandoned this ambition. Instead, he gave help, practical assistance and money to those earnestly engaged in an attempt to change the climate of opinion. He had come to recognise the power of ideas and knew that an intellectual sea-change was necessary if policies with the potential to reverse Britain's decline were to become politically acceptable. As on subsequent occasions, Vinson found himself siding with a small minority of intellectuals bent on challenging the prevailing orthodoxy, even if the means by which he reached his conclusions – intuition combined with a constant process of reflecting privately on experience and events – may have been different from theirs.

The IEA, of which he was later to become chairman and life vice-president, had been founded in 1955 by an eccentric old Etonian. Anthony Fisher, an entrepreneur and ex-Battle of Britain pilot, had made a fortune from chicken farming and went on to lose another fortune farming turtles in the Cayman Islands. Like Vinson, he had abandoned the ambition to become an MP in order to help change the political weather. It turned out the year 1972 would be an important turning point in Vinson's life: it was the year in which he stood down as CEO of Plastic Coatings; the year in which he got married; and the year in which Fisher persuaded Vinson to become an IEA trustee.

Described many years later by Andrew Marr as the most successful think tank in history, the IEA was run by two economists – Ralph Harris and Arthur Seldon – whose fearless assault on the economic establishment was conducted with flair, gusto and a contrarian spirit to match Vinson's own. Vinson gave money at a stage in the IEA's history when finances were precarious and survival was uncertain. He also steered other potential sources of funds and influence in the think tank's direction. Later on, as chairman of the board, he was to save the IEA from collapse, after internal feuds erupted into newspaper columns.

The invitation to join the board had followed an invitation to lunch at the institute's offices in Lord North Street, which was prompted by a letter from Vinson to the *Daily Telegraph* about economic issues. Impressed by the scale of the institute's ambition and the quality of its work, Vinson provided a loan of £100,000, from which the organisation derived around £10,000 per year in interest. At the time, the top marginal tax rate was 98 per cent, so a loan of this kind was a more efficient form of funding than an outright gift would have been: 'Ralph asked me what security I needed. I said that none was required. We shook hands on the arrangement, and I wrote out the cheque. I got my money back when the IEA's funding was sufficiently strong to permit repayment.'

Vinson has made many grants to the IEA over the years and remains a major donor.

The IEA's aims were set out in its first promotional brochure, which stated that the sole concern would be 'economic truth', un-swayed by political considerations. Its ultimate objective would be a society in which people would understand free-market economics, 'together with an understanding of the moral foundations which govern the acquisition and holding of property and the necessity of a secure and honest monetary system'. The new institute also promised to make the works of the great classical liberal economists more widely available.

The moral dimension implicit in the IEA's mission

statement and the family atmosphere that existed in the IEA's offices in Westminster – which, in many ways, made it resemble a small family business – would undoubtedly have appealed to Vinson. Both his instincts and his experience as a businessman distinguished him from the free-market advocates who believed that self-interest and price mechanism alone were sufficient to ensure satisfactory economic outcomes – an attitude parodied in the Hollywood film *Wall Street*, when broker Gordon Gekko famously declared 'Greed is good!'

Like Ralph Harris – a strong Christian whose moral outlook was described by *The Spectator* as that of 'a traditional Protestant, more sin and sorrowful than joy in resurrection' – Vinson inclines to the view that economies only flourish when they are grounded in a strong sense of public morality. Vinson took an instant liking to Harris, and was impressed by his energy and flair. The engaging personality of the latter – very different from that of most professional economists – impressed many, as a growing number of people sought his advice.

Richard Cockett, in his book *Thinking the Unthinkable*, sums it up:

> Although there was nothing remotely false about Harris, few would have guessed his north London origins.

A slim, elegant pipe-smoking figure with a Bertie Wooster haircut, usually sporting an embroidered waistcoat and possessor of a remarkable collection of hats, Harris could almost have passed as a member of the aristocracy. But the tenacity with which he was to assault the prevailing economic orthodoxy, and the obvious relish with which he did so, may have owed a great deal to his background. As he later acknowledged: 'I had a bit of a chip on my shoulder. If I met public school boys I would mock their accents, because these were the people who would condescend to help workers along with little state hand-outs and subsidies and benefits!'

The Harris-Seldon partnership, which lasted for thirty years, worked well because, in the words of the American Nobel prize-winning economist Milton Freedman:

They complemented one another – they fitted together like pieces in a jigsaw puzzle. Ralph, outgoing hail-fellow-well-met, an excellent public speaker, was an ideal choice for the 'outside'. Arthur was an exacting academic with a passion for precision, the ideal choice for the 'inside' role. Ralph was a brilliant voice for the institute: Arthur an unrelenting enforcer of intellectual standards in the institute's books and the celebrated Hobart papers he created. Ralph's interest in the politics of economics balanced Arthur's in the economics of politics.

The achievement of the IEA has been widely acknowledged – as Cockett continues:

> By the mid-1970s ... the IEA had, over the course of more than twenty years, developed a body of free-market ideas applicable to all areas of the economy. They had developed a coherent set of principles, the principles of economic liberalism, applicable to a modern economy, thus fulfilling Hayek's 1947 hope that the economic liberals would refine and develop liberalism into a modern, vibrant philosophy ... The IEA's greatest achievement was to develop and publicise a modern programme of economic liberalism unrivalled in the world.[3]

A year after becoming an IEA trustee, Harris introduced Vinson to Sir Keith Joseph, who asked him to help him set

---

3 Richard Cockett, *Thinking the Unthinkable: Think tanks and the Economic Counter-Revolution 1931–83*, Harper Collins, 1995.

Nettlestead Place, Kent, where Nigel was born. His father Ronald, here pictured in 1965, was crippled with ageing hips.

Nigel's mother Bettina ice-skating in Lenzerheide, Switzerland, 1937.

Nigel's mother demonstrating to women of the WI how to use a stirrup pump to extinguish incendiary fires anticipated in 1940.

Bettina with her two sons Mark (aged five, *left*) and Nigel (aged two, *right*).

A lover of horses throughout his life: Nigel on Dapples at Beckett's Farm, Romney Marsh, 1937 (*left*) and on Woody in 1986 (*right*).

Nigel, aged sixteen, proudly showing off the first radio he had built (*left*). This was a hobby that was to prove profoundly useful to him throughout his industrial life; two years later, while awaiting call-up, he built a radio room from army war surplus equipment (*right*).

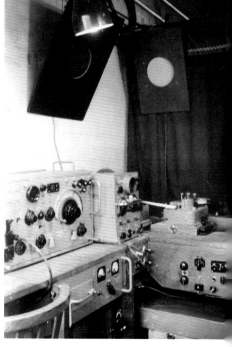

Nigel, aged thirteen, as a cadet in his first year at Pangbourne College (*left*) and then, aged nineteen, newly commissioned into the Queen's Royal Regiment before his posting to Egypt (*right*).

The beginning: the first factory in Friary Square, Guildford, in 1952. The cars weren't Nigel's!

Nigel among products awaiting a corrosion-proof coating at the Guildford factory in 1958.

Nigel Vinson:
aspiring young
businessman
in 1965.

Receiving the Queen's
Award for Technical
Innovation from the
Lord Lieutenant of
Surrey, 1971.

Nigel, as chairman of
the Rural Development
Commission, meeting
with the Cleveland
Planning and
Development Committ
in 1985 as part of his
regular tours to promot
rural enterprise.

Roddam Hall before (1971, *top*) and after (1974, *above*) Nigel's conversion.

Nigel's marriage to Yvonne in 1972.

Nigel with the Prince of Wales at the launch of the
re-named Rural Development Commission. The Prince
was being introduced to Mrs Batty Shaw (a fellow
commissioner) as Yvonne smiles in the background.

With Yvonne, gifting a village green to
Holborn, Northumberland, 2004.

Keith Joseph finds happiness at last: his reception at Roddam after marrying Yolanda, 16 August 1990.

The three daughters: Nonie (*left*), Rowena (*centre*) and Bettina (*right*) in 1990. In the background is a tapestry of tulips by Elizabeth Blackadder, commissioned from the Dovecot Studio, Edinburgh.

The house of his
dreams: Roddam Rigg.
Nigel, aged eighty,
was its architect,
surveyor and building
supervisor.

Nigel and Yvonne in
retirement at Roddam
Rigg, 2014

Nigel in robes in
2012, painted by
Frances Bell.

up a think tank with the aim of taking the IEA's arguments more directly into the political arena. It was important that the two organisations got along and there should not be an unseemly competition for funds. Harris later told friends that he had 'given Nigel to Keith' as a gesture of goodwill and to signal the IEA's willingness to cooperate with the new organisation.

It was a gift that was greatly appreciated: Vinson's background as an entrepreneur – along with his evident energy, supremely practical nature and political commitment – recommended him to Joseph. The two men became firm friends and Nigel was subsequently asked to act as Joseph's best man when he remarried in 1990 as well as being the executor of Joseph's will following his death in 1994 – a task that turned out to be more onerous when the will was contested by Joseph's first wife.

Vinson attributes the fact he turned out to be a perfect fit in his new role (treasurer and linkman to the IEA) as a fine example of happenstance – the happy outcome of chance and circumstance.

Today, the role of the entrepreneur is far better understood than it was in the mid-1970s, when few people even knew what the word meant. At the time, Joseph frequently lamented the fact that the literal translation of the term from the French was 'undertaker'. He even engaged in

earnest discussion with intellectual allies about whether
a more sympathetic word could be found to describe the
function of business risk-takers, to whom Joseph ascribed
near-heroic status and whose importance, he believed, was
being overlooked. In a speech on the crucial role of the
entrepreneur, Joseph declared:

> We must understand the role of the decision-makers,
> the entrepreneur or risk-takers. The market in its con-
> stant adjustment to changing public demand is a world
> of uncertainty. It is the entrepreneur who identifies a
> demand and, subject to competition within the law,
> in the hope of profit, seeks to satisfy it. In order to do
> so, he or she orchestrates skills, machinery, materials,
> money. Without entrepreneurs, the system will not work.

Vinson, in Joseph's view, was quite evidently a man who
could make things work and, in the event, orchestrated
the skills, resources and money necessary to create a new
think tank – the CPS. Within weeks of their initial meeting
in the early part of 1974, Vinson had found premises: a
terraced Georgian house at 8 Wilfred Street SW1, which
turned out to be ideal for the purposes of intellectual persuasion – the task Joseph had set for it. Nigel also designed
the letterhead, hired the staff and underwrote the lease.

According to the stationery, its declared aim was: 'to secure fuller understanding of the methods to improve the standard of living, the quality of life and the freedom of choice of the British people, with particular attention to social market policies'. It would fly the Tory flag but would be separate from, and independent of, the party's policy-making processes.

On nearly all of the important economic issues of the day, Vinson already held views that were to be associated with Thatcherism. Indeed, in several important respects he can even claim to have been a Thatcherite before Thatcher herself.

Analysts have disagreed about the exact nature of Thatcherism. Perhaps the most persuasive account has been given by the philosopher Shirley Letwin, who argued that it was an attitude, not a policy, and that its essence was a moral agenda to promote the so-called 'vigorous virtues' – qualities that needed to be cultivated if Britain, at that particular moment in history, were to cease laughing at itself and begin to recover from its malaise.

Letwin wrote:

> Although the Thatcherite conception of the individual has never been announced in a single soliloquy at centre stage, or indeed ever articulated, it has been the

clear, though implicit, theme of a series of speeches, policies and acts. After fifteen years of the rhetoric and practise of Thatcherism, its outlines are clear. The individual preferred by Thatcherism is to begin with a simple list: upright, self-sufficient, energetic, adventurous, independent-minded, loyal to friends, and robust against enemies.

These are qualities that – as Vinson's friends and associates will attest – he possesses in abundance. Vinson was a Thatcherite man *par excellence*; these qualities, combined with charm and persuasiveness, helped facilitate measures designed to unleash the energies and talents of those with similar qualities, thus ending – and then reversing – Britain's decline.

Early descriptions of the centre's aims and objectives, to which Vinson made suggestions and contributions, stressed that great attention would be paid to the policies of other western countries – those whose economic performances had outstripped Britain's – in the hope that important lessons might be learned.

In reality, such statements were intended to persuade Edward Heath that Joseph and his associates would be engaged in a harmless intellectual exercise, thus assuaging any anxieties the then Tory leader may have had about the CPS formulating an alternative direction in terms of policy – and consequently presenting a challenge to his leadership. It was a rare example of Joseph being less than open with his Cabinet colleagues. In a statement timed to coincide with the announcement of the centre's launch, Mr Heath said that he had invited Sir Keith, as part of his shadow Cabinet duties, to look into 'the contribution that private enterprise has made to the high standard of living and the steadily improving social services of many other countries'.[4]

In a further attempt to assuage Heath's anxieties, they asked him to nominate his own representative to the CPS board. As it happened, no attention was given to the business of comparative economic research and Adam Ridley, the young economist nominated by Heath, failed to prevent the CPS from developing an alternative economic and industrial policy.

In this enterprise, Joseph had the support of his vice-chairman Margaret Thatcher and a voluble, eccentric ex-communist from the East End of London called Alfred Sherman, who had fought in the Spanish Civil War and, as the centre's director of research, played a large part in determining the CPS's direction and priorities.

---

4 *The Times,* 15 January 1975.

The IEA and the CPS were remarkably complementary. According to Sherman: 'Had it not been for the IEA there would have been no Thatcher revolution of the 1970s and '80s – *pace* Enoch Powell – the voice crying in the wilderness.'

His spell at the CPS taught Vinson never to underestimate the influence of the Jewish lobby.

The task of the CPS was to persuade the Conservative Party to abandon the political middle ground it had occupied during the Heath years. Adopting free-market policies would help facilitate the necessary change of philosophy by influencing opinion-formers in the media and academia – without the inhibitions of conventional views about what was politically possible. As Sherman put it:

> The centre – it was agreed – was to act as 'outsider', 'skirmisher', 'trail blazer' to moot new ideas and policies without committing the party leadership; in the hope that sufficient headway had been made with public opinion and inside the party, the leadership could move forward. Our job was to question the unquestioned, think the unthinkable, blaze new trails.

Vinson's involvement with both organisations ensured that they continued to play complementary roles. The scale of the IEA and the CPS's achievement has been widely acknowledged; the proliferation of think tanks in the UK and throughout the Anglosphere since the 1970s is a reflection of their success. It tends to be forgotten that, in their early days, both organisations were regarded as objects of ridicule or derision, an attitude that became outright hostility in some quarters as their ideas took hold and their influence grew. Involvement in the organisations' activities required independence of mind and entailed reputational risk. Most of those engaged in the work of the IEA and the CPS were natural outsiders.

Vinson, the son of a gentleman farmer, had become an outsider as the result of conviction and temperament. There was no doubting Vinson's ambition, or his desire to make a significant contribution to public life, but it was also clear that he was not prepared to modify his opinions for the sake of his career or the good opinion of Britain's business and political leaders, with whom he was at odds intellectually. Given that he had no formal training in economics and left school at seventeen, it was difficult not to be impressed by his self-assurance – a quality apparent from an early age – as well as his clear grasp of essentials. He advised business colleagues: 'Make your decisions intuitively, then back them up factually.' Vinson approached economic and political issues in a similar way.

I am – as author – indebted to Nigel Vinson and Alfred Sherman for having recruited me to the CPS staff in October 1974. As a young researcher, and subsequently a member of the CPS board, I was able to witness the growing conflict between Tory softline 'Wets' and hardline 'Dries' as Joseph abandoned the political middle ground – which he had once occupied with distinction – in favour of market-based policies and measures designed to defend individual liberty from trade union power and big government.

'It was only in April 1974 that I was converted to conservatism,' Joseph declared in 1975. This was a view that surprised, and even dismayed, many of those who had served with him in the Heath government. He continued: 'I had thought that I was a Conservative but now I see that I was not really one at all.'

Such sentiments did not endear him to the Tory front bench.

Vinson's CPS role was to bring in the money, but there was virtually no aspect of the centre's work in which he did not involve himself. His deeply practical nature, thoughtfulness and enthusiasm helped build a congenial working environment and reduced the risk of the centre fracturing from the impact of competing egos and doctrinal squabbles. Vinson was also chairman of one of the centre's most influential and successful study groups, which produced proposals for pension reform, personal savings and business start-ups that were later adopted by the Thatcher government – and which came to affect the lives of millions.

Potential donors who came for lunch at the centre's small dining room on Wilfred Street were impressed by Joseph's high-mindedness and intellectuality and by Vinson's charm, sincerity and selfless commitment, even if a significant number may have been discouraged from reaching for their cheque books by Sherman's tendency to insult those whose views he judged to be lacking in intellectual rigour. Since this included a high proportion of those invited, stratagems were sometimes devised to ensure that particularly important guests were invited on days when Alfred was expected to be absent.

Sherman's choice of targets was remarkably catholic and included members of the shadow Cabinet. His insults quickly became the stuff of political gossip, but they made Vinson's fundraising task more difficult. Nevertheless, a stream of rigorous, well-researched speeches and publications helped redefine the Conservative Party's philosophy and future direction.

With Martin Wassell, recruited by Vinson to act as the centre's general director, he co-authored the centre's first publication – *Why Britain Needs a Social Market Economy* – which came to be known by those who worked for the CPS as 'the credo'. Its purpose, according to a foreword written by Keith Joseph, was to reconsider the conventional wisdom and 'to approach our social market philosophy with fresh eyes'.

The pamphlet defined social market economy as a 'socially responsible market economy, for a market economy is perfectly compatible with a more compassionate society. Indeed, by encouraging the energies and initiative of the creative and sturdier members of society our resources for helping the aged, the sick and the disabled are substantially enlarged.'

The publication had two other key messages. Firstly, that the market was: 'the most efficient mechanism the world has ever known for performing the bewildering task of coordinating the efforts and desires of the millions of individuals that constitute a complex industrialised society.' Secondly, that economic freedom was a necessary, if not sufficient, condition for political freedom. What the country was suffering from, the authors concluded, was not a crisis of capitalism – as the socialists alleged – but a crisis of government intervention in the market.

It is a measure of the influence of the IEA and the CPS that, forty years on, almost nothing in *Why Britain Needs a Social Market Economy* strikes the contemporary reader as controversial.

Sometime after its publication, Joseph ceased to use the phrase 'social market economy', having been persuaded by the Letwins that the phrase diluted the understanding of market economics and failed to acknowledge the primacy of economic forces. Although little separated Joseph and Vinson in terms of what needed to be done to arrest Britain's decline, Vinson continued to use the term as, in his view, it was important to stress the social benefits of the market order and its participative character.

When, in 1974–75, Joseph agonised over whether to run for the leadership of the Conservative Party, Vinson was one of a small number of people Joseph consulted to see if they thought he possessed the necessary qualities to be Prime Minister. Vinson advised against him standing. It was not that Joseph was incapable of making decisions; rather, Vinson judged that the personal trauma through which Joseph put himself before reaching an important decision was simply too debilitating for him to stand the strains and pressures of the highest office. This view was indeed borne out when Joseph later suffered a series of nerve-based health problems when serving in the Thatcher Cabinet.

Vinson also believed that Joseph was seriously handicapped by his first wife Helen's ill-concealed distaste for politics, and her refusal to give the kind of support that wives of front-bench Tory politicians customarily provided. An internal memo, penned by Vinson shortly after the launch of the CPS, described Joseph as 'courteous, charming, and endlessly frazzled from a ghastly home life due to a wholly unsupportive wife'. The note continued: 'Subsequently I advised him [Joseph] that he would kill himself if he attempted to be Prime Minister. Much better to be Chancellor or [to hold] some other post rather than carrying the top responsibility.'

The note acknowledged Joseph's 'incredible mind and memory' but recognised that his intellectual agonising stifled his natural intuition. The result was that his constant search for the truth – 'and the Holy Grail of the ultimate solutions' – resulted in endless disputations and fact-finding missions that 'substituted for decision taking until the very last moment'.

Vinson's advice that his friend should not stand for party leadership appears to have strengthened Joseph's own doubts about his suitability for the highest office; he certainly had no subsequent regrets about not seeking leadership. 'Had I become leader,' Joseph told the historian Anthony Seldon before the 1987 general election, 'it would have been a disaster for the party, [for the] country and for me.'

On one issue – interest rates – Joseph and Vinson

disagreed repeatedly, over a period of several years. During the years immediately following the creation of the CPS, inflation peaked at 27 per cent and many feared that Britain could face a South American-style hyperinflation – an anxiety that, at this stage, was shared by Margaret Thatcher, the new Conservative leader. Joseph, as well as his allies at the IEA, argued that inflation was essentially a monetary phenomenon: while bringing the money supply under control was not a miracle cure for Britain's economic difficulties, it was a necessary condition in finding solutions to a range of economic problems.

Some of this newly fashionable monetarist thinking even rubbed off on the Bank of England and the Labour government. During Denis Healey's Chancellorship, the Bank restored the publication of monetary aggregates; meanwhile, Callaghan sounded the death knell of his neo-Keynesian policies of seeking full employment through the management of demand in a famous speech to his party's annual conference written by his son-in-law, economist Peter Jay.

High interest rates, which in those days were set by the Treasury rather than the Bank of England, were increasingly seen as the key element in an effective anti-inflationary policy. As a former industrialist and member of the CBI Council, Vinson pointed repeatedly to the problems experienced as a consequence of high rates. He argued that they poured oil on the flames of wage demands as workers found their ever-increasing mortgages impossible to service. Joseph, on the other hand, supported by Sherman, argued that historically high rates of interest were necessary to reduce inflation and that to force down such rates would penalise savers.

Inflation began to fall following the Conservative victory of 1979, but it still remained stubbornly in double digits. Interest rates were the key element of the government's medium-term financial strategy but stayed at historically high levels. So too did the official figures for money supply, although its measurement was fraught with a range of technical difficulties and it was not clear which of the available means of measuring money supply was the most appropriate guide for policy. The inevitable consequence of high rates was a strong pound, which made life difficult for business and acutely difficult for exporters.

Interest rates rose to 17 per cent in November 1979, making the pound worth $2.4 – 21 per cent above its purchasing power parity. Vinson knew this level would have a devastating impact on Britain's ability to export and he made certain that Joseph, now Secretary for Industry, was aware of the problem. Having consulted other industrialists he had met in the CBI and who shared his concerns, Vinson arranged for one of them, the CEO of Lansing Bagnall (a manufacturer of forklift trucks based near Basingstoke), to have a personal meeting with Joseph. Vinson said later:

> He arrived with a plethora of really well worked-out charts showing how the over-valued pound had made large sections of British industry uncompetitive, not least his own. Joseph was impressed, but when I talked to him subsequently, he said: 'Nigel, there is nothing I can do about it. Geoffrey is the man to see. Rising interest rates is very much part of his policy of bringing inflation under control.'

The fate of Lansing Bagnall was not untypical of a substantial section of British manufacturing industry. As orders declined, the company was taken over by the German company Linde AG in late 1989 and much of its remaining production was moved from the UK to France and Germany. The Basingstoke factory ceased production entirely in 2010.

Vinson believes Thatcher would have heeded his advice, along with similar entreaties from others, but for the stubborn persistence of her Chancellor, a lawyer with no background in business or industry. Thatcher's instincts, which in this instance did not prevail, were a sounder basis for policy than Howe's stubborn adherence to economic doctrine, which was – what came to be referred to as – 'sado-monetarism'.

Thatcher's memoirs make it clear that, as a general rule, she was opposed to high interest rates unless they could be proven to be absolutely essential, rather than imposed for political reasons: 'High interest rates do ensure a high, real reward for savers. But they discourage risk-taking and self-improvement. In the long run, they are a force for stagnation rather than enterprise. For that reason I was against putting up rates unless it was necessary.'

Vinson therefore appeared vindicated in laying the burden of blame at the door of Howe for a monetary policy he now believes contributed to a thirty-year decline in manufacturing. It is also clear that others came round to his view that interest rates were too high. These others included: Sir Alan Walters, who was brought in as Mrs Thatcher's economic adviser in 1981; John Hoskyns, the head of her policy unit; and Alfred Sherman, with whom Vinson had previously disagreed on the subject of interest rates. All of these men now concluded that interest rates were significantly too high during Howe's Chancellorship. It seemed even the toughest-minded monetarists believed that the medicine being administered to the ailing British economy was too severe. Vinson later commented: 'It taught me that no economic theory looks watertight ten years after it is fashionable.'

In office, Mrs Thatcher argued that the medicine administered by her first government *was* necessary and frequently used the phrase 'there is no alternative' (a claim repeated so often that it came to be known by the acronym TINA). We now know that, in the case of interest rates, this was not strictly true – as Mrs Thatcher herself later acknowledged. Unlike Joseph, her guide and intellectual mentor, Thatcher was not apt to admit error. But she did later write:

> Alan Walters, John Hoskyns and Alfred Sherman had suggested that Professor Jürg Niehans, a distinguished Swiss monetarist economist, should prepare a study on our monetary policy for me. Professor Niehans' report which I read in early February [1981], though framed in highly technical language, had a clear message. It was that North Sea oil had probably not been a major factor in sterling's appreciation, rather, tight monetary policy had caused the pound to rise imposing such pressure on British industry and deepening the recession ... In short, Professor Niehans thought that monetary policy was too tight and should be quickly loosened.

As John Hoskyns later noted, the Niehans paper advocated measures that could be seen as the government publicly admitting they had, albeit mistakenly, done the economy a great deal of damage. As inflation fell, monetary policy was loosened in the way that Professor Niehans recommended, although, in Vinson's view, it was not loosened fast or far enough, and the consequence – a diminished industrial base – remains with us.

Vinson is not an economist, although he does have a clear understanding of monetarist theory and has contributed hugely to the work of the IEA and the CPS – the two UK organisations that have done the most to explain the monetary roots of inflation. He is also familiar with the controversies over which measurement of money is the most reliable when setting interest rates. But he is not an absolutist, and where common sense collides with theory – which, in his view, was what happened in Britain in the early 1980s – he is apt to vote for common sense.

However, it does not automatically follow that, in urging lower interest over many years, Vinson was invariably right. The 'right rate' varies according to economic circumstances – a subject that is bound to be a matter of dispute among economists. Nevertheless, it is clear that, had Vinson's advice been heeded at that critical moment in British history, the damage done to industry could have been significantly reduced. Unemployment, which peaked at more than three million (12.2 per cent) in 1984, would not have reached the same historically high levels, nor would the bitterness caused by Thatcherism in some sections of society have been as deep or long-lasting.

More than a quarter of a century later, Vinson was to write in *Standpoint*:

> It has been argued that one of Geoffrey Howe's great successes was to let the pound float and be freely adjusted according to market forces. But this is a myth as, in reality, the value of the pound is significantly influenced by the bank rate. If this contributes to keeping the value of sterling well above its purchasing power, then businesses whose profit margins are seldom much more than 10 per cent inevitably become uncompetitive. For a trading nation like Britain to ignore the value at which it trades – the value of sterling – can now be seen as an error of the first magnitude. It decimated our industrial framework, gave us a massive imbalance of trade and huge international borrowings, all of which had to be serviced by an ever-increasing burden of general taxation.

This disagreement between Vinson and other leading Thatcherites should not detract from the achievement of the CPS, which was to change the economic philosophy of the Conservative Party. It did this by bringing about a major watershed in the history of post-war British politics and, in the process, discrediting the economic concepts on which socialism is based. 'The Centre for Policy Studies was where our Conservative revolution began,' Margaret Thatcher said later. 'I do think we have accomplished the revival of the philosophy and principles of a free society. We set up the Centre for Policy Studies, and it has propagated those ideas, and they have been accepted.'

When Vinson resigned as treasurer of the CPS to become chairman of the RDC in 1980, Margaret Thatcher wrote to him:

> What has been achieved during the past six years by way of winning the intellectual argument in favour of free enterprise and against socialism and corporatism would never have been possible without your patient guidance and tireless ability to provide, and then maintain, the foundation stone upon which we have built. I am, and will always be, immensely grateful to you. Your contribution was invaluable.

10 DOWNING STREET

28th July 1980

Dear Nigel,

Thank you very much indeed for your kind letter of 15th July.

What has been achieved during the past six years by way
of winning the intellectual argument in favour of free
enterprise and against socialism and corporatism would never
have been possible without your patient guidance
and tireless ability to provide, and then maintain,
the foundation stone upon which we have built. I am,
and will always be, immensely grateful to you.
Your contribution was invaluable.

I was so pleased that you were able to accept the new
job. The Centre will miss you, but the Commission is
fortunate to secure your many and proven talents.
I could not agree more with your excellent letter in the
Times on Friday.

With best wishes,

Nigel Vinson Esq MVO

Nigel retired as treasurer of the CPS but remained
chairman of the Wider Capital Formation Group.

Throughout his years at the CPS, Vinson was keen to ensure that the IEA receive full credit for turning the tide of economic and political opinion.

Later, Ralph Harris's seventieth birthday prompted Nigel to compose a poem – typical of Nigel's occasional verses in its mix of good humour, playfulness and puns – that contained the following lines:

Let every trumpet toot
His birthday to salute
The amusing and astute
Head of our institute
History cannot efface
Due to his intellect and grace
The world's a freer place
His personal conviction
Led to socialist eviction
His crushing passion
Put markets back in fashion
We are richer by the mile
For his life enhancing style
Half serious with a smile
Dear Ralph – This message comes from many men –
God bless your three score years and ten.

Harris was delighted with the poem and declared himself astounded that Nigel should have written it.

In a personal letter to Arthur Seldon and his wife Marjorie, on the occasion of Arthur's eightieth birthday, Nigel wrote: 'To have helped change the history of our times as you have done is a contribution, I believe, the world will never forget.'

A year after agreeing to help Margaret Thatcher and Keith Joseph establish the CPS, Nigel Vinson took a lead role in running another highly ambitious initiative: the Queen's Silver Jubilee Appeal.

The invitation to head the appeal had come in 1974, when Vinson had lunched with Sir Michael Hawkins, a near neighbour and the Duke of Gloucester's equerry. Hawkins had asked Nigel to help him run the forthcoming Jubilee appeal, to be built on the existing fabric of the King George's Jubilee Trust. Vinson approved strongly of the aim of the appeal: to express, in a lasting manner, the nation's affection for the Queen and its gratitude for her dedicated service over twenty-five years. The idea was to launch the appeal in December 1975 with Prince Charles as chairman. Vinson therefore accepted immediately, but explained that, because of other commitments, he could only work two days a week – and would only accept the position on an unpaid basis. In the event, the job took two and a half days a week and lasted for three years.

As honorary director of the Queen's Silver Jubilee Appeal, he not only provided strategy, organisational advice and a hands-on role in setting up national and local fundraising committees, but he also helped shape the appeal's scope and character. With the Queen's consent, it had been agreed from the start that the funds raised would assist youth organisations. It was also suggested that a phrase often attributed to King George VI – 'tomorrow belongs to them' – could be usefully employed during the period of the appeal. Realising, however, that the occasion should embrace the interest and sympathies of everyone, not just young people, Hawkins agreed with Vinson's view that the appeal's real purpose should be the encouragement of young people to serve the wider community. They devised the slogan: 'to help young people to help others'. Through officials, Nigel learned that the Queen agreed this was more outward-looking and purposeful.

Vinson quickly realised that the organisation's offices in St James would be inadequate for a national appeal on the scale proposed and he immediately identified more suitable premises at 8 Buckingham Gate. Fearing that the appeal would be gazumped unless he acted quickly, he loaned the deposit on the premises out of his own pocket – just as he had done at the CPS. Four years later, when the work of the appeal was done, the premises were sold at a profit of more than £100,000.

His next step was to place an advertisement in *The Times* for a full-time appeal secretary and he interviewed the applicants himself. The job went to William Chalmers, who proved meticulous and dedicated.

Using his contacts at the Design Centre, Nigel asked Milner Gray, a leading industrial designer, to produce a logo for the appeal. The logo was approved by the Queen, with copyrights collected by the Design Council on behalf of the appeal.

During this period, Nigel spent one day a week in the office and a second day visiting major counties throughout the country where he met councillors, mayors, church leaders and anyone else able, qualified and willing to form local fundraising committees. This culminated in a special address to the Lord-Lieutenants during their annual conference at St James's.

Although hugely successful, the appeal placed a considerable strain on those responsible for coordinating the diverse groups involved, not least Sir Michael Hawkins, who was found dead by Nigel at his desk following a heart attack in May 1976.

Following Sir Michael's death, contact with the palace became more tenuous since Prince Charles was often on duty at sea with the Royal Navy. Nigel had, however, formed a deep respect for him – although he remarked to friends that the Prince's views on alternative medicine might be sounder if he knew more science. Relations with the Prince were largely conducted through his equerry David Check-etts, a bit of a rough Australian diamond, who, when asked by one of the secretaries what the gardens of Buckingham Palace were like, memorably replied: 'All flamingos and corgi shit.'

As the appeal drew to a conclusion, Vinson commis-sioned Gerald Benney, a leading silversmith he had known during his time at the Design Council, to come up with a set of souvenir port coasters, incorporating the Silver Jubi-lee Appeal medal. When presenting them to the Prince on behalf of the appeal team, Nigel employed one of his outrageous puns: 'Sir, during your naval career you have been more used to sea-based coasters, but I hope that the enclosed coasters, which are intended to be land-based, may give you equal pleasure and may they be a lasting memento.'

Although Vinson found the work of running the appeal

rewarding, it is clear that the Prince had ample reason to be grateful to him too. The result of the appeal was outstanding: it raised £14.6 million – at that time, the largest sum ever raised on behalf of a charitable appeal, and equivalent to more than £100 million in today's money.

After initial allocations, the balance was transferred to the Prince's Youth Business Trust to support its work encouraging young entrepreneurs – a cause dear to Vinson's heart and one he had vigorously promoted through his involvement at the CPS and as chairman of the RDC. Twenty years later, as the result of a further coincidence, he was to become chairman of the north-east branch of the Prince's Youth Business Trust, a position that enabled him to make constructive use of the money he had helped raise.

Vinson's work as honorary director of the Queen's Silver Jubilee Appeal was subsequently rewarded when he was made a Lieutenant of the Victorian Order. His friends, however, did not think this truly matched the scale of his contribution.

CHAPTER 6

Building a rural life-support machine

U NTIL NIGEL VINSON was made chairman of the Development Commission by Margaret Thatcher in 1980, planning requirements made it virtually impossible to create a business in one's own home. This was a constraint that pressed particularly hard upon those living in the countryside, who might otherwise have made a living through the manufacture and sale of craftwork and farm produce. Small rural businesses were also handicapped by restrictions that prevented them from erecting signs to attract customers. These, and similar constraints, accentuated the decline of the rural economy, which was already shedding jobs due to the relentless – but nationally beneficial – gains in agricultural efficiency. The life prospects of some 10 per cent of the English population who lived in the countryside at that time were diminishing.

Certainly, as Nigel Vinson took up his new role, there was little sign in Westminster or Whitehall of a realistic vision to arrest the decline of rural communities. A mood of pessimism about their future generally prevailed as it became increasingly accepted that individuals, not the government, created jobs.

The Development Commission, renamed the Rural Development Commission in 1982 at Vinson's suggestion, was one of Britain's oldest quangos, having been created in 1909, when the mechanisation of agriculture was accelerating the drift of population from villages to towns and cities. Its purpose was to promote the economic interests of those living in the countryside and, in particular, to increase the number and variety of jobs.

Nigel Vinson was exceptionally well suited for his new role, and was subsequently reappointed to the post – which he enjoyed over a period of ten years. His knowledge and sympathetic understanding of the problems of small businesses – whose cause he had long championed – paired with his love of the countryside – which went back to his childhood in rural, pre-war Kent – made him an inspired choice. He also had the advantage of having a clear grasp of the new Tory government's economic priorities, as well as Cabinet-level contacts, experience of running a 3,000-acre Northumberland farm and knowledge of raising a family in a small rural community.

In addition, Vinson, who was chairman of the Crafts Council of Great Britain[5] from 1962, still has a love of craftwork and an admiration for the patience and skill of those who engage in it that communicates itself immediately when he talks on the subject.

The Development Commission chairmanship, previously occupied by former Labour MP Lord Northfield, was a paid position, but Vinson insisted that he would only take on the job in an honorary capacity. If his new colleagues at the commission took this as evidence that he wished to perform the role in a distant, hands-off manner – the style of the well-born English amateur – they were quickly disabused of this notion by the energy, knowledge and purpose Nigel brought

---

5 Later renamed the Crafts Council.

to his task. He explained his disinclination to draw a salary by simply saying he did not believe those sufficiently well-off needed payment for public service.

Vinson's natural impatience for results, and his frustration with bureaucratic procedures, meant he was not a typical quango appointee. He had, however, already served on another quango – the Sugar Board – although he had concluded it served no useful purpose whatever and advised it should be closed down. This advice may well have influenced the government's decision to scrap the Sugar Board in 1975.

Vinson's first task as chairman, having been a member of the commission since 1979, was to assess just how effective the organisation was and to report his findings to Tom King, the Minister for Local Government and Environmental Services. He wrote to King in August 1980:

> I have now been in the job for three months and have had a good opportunity to take an overall look at the activities and achievements of the commission and its agents. You asked me to give you a frank opinion on the organisation, and I think I can best sum up the position by saying that I find a state of 'benign confusion'. On the whole, the staff are competent, keen and committed, but there is delay, frustration and

wastefulness caused by wholly unnecessary bureaucracy. The complexity of this 'grown like Topsy'
structure means that the Development Commission
cannot carry out its remit as satisfactorily as it could.

Vinson told the minister that he had asked himself whether
there was still a need for the commission and concluded
with 'a qualified yes':

> There is still a need – perhaps stronger than ever – for
> an independent rural voice to advise the government
> objectively about the special problems of rural areas.
> Also the commission has a most useful role as a goad
> – encouraging other bodies to do things that they
> would not otherwise do, and it is the only organisa-
> tion looking at rural problems across a broad front
> – economic and social.

Vinson's review, which also covered the role of other public
agencies and institutions concerned with the development
of the rural economy, went on to paint a picture of wastefulness, missed opportunities, organisational overlap,
duplication of services, unnecessary regulation and a system of Whitehall oversight that delayed decision-making
and frustrated the commission's staff.

Vinson, as a countryman, realised the economic harm done to outdoor workers when the clocks went back unnecessarily and outside work was curtailed. So, through the commission, he organised an England-wide poll that asked over 5,000 people for their views; 72 per cent were in favour of longer evenings and this was heavily endorsed by the Sports Council, tourist agencies, golf course managers, the self-employed and, not least, Help the Aged, who were concerned that old people were virtually curfewed by three o'clock in the middle of winter as they were afraid to be out in the dark. His campaign was supported widely in the press and in both Houses of Parliament, but it was knocked on the head by the Home Office through fear of upsetting the Scots. This sort of broad-brush initiative to help rural areas was, alas, easier said than done.

He was ahead of his time in trying to persuade supermarkets and other retail food chains to introduce special counters featuring locally grown produce – an idea received sympathetically at the time (1985) by Lord Sieff of Marks & Spencer, but one that has taken many years to fructify.

Some of Vinson's other proposals for reform could not subsequently be acted on either. He failed, for example, to win the commission the same freedom of action enjoyed by the Welsh and Scottish development agencies.

But he did introduce a series of changes and initiatives to streamline decision-making and reduce bureaucracy. The most significant organisational change occurred with the merger of the commission with its main agency, the Council for Small Industries in Rural Areas (CoSIRA), in 1988. Prince Charles very much approved of the change and hosted a reception at St James's Palace to demonstrate his support.

Vinson also phased out the advanced factory-building programme because the same task was already performed by another quango, English Estates, and because he could see no reason for the job to be done by one body in the towns and another in the country:

> When I informed the DoI [Department of Industry] that I was happy to divest my powers in this area, they were rather surprised and said that I was the first quango boss ever to suggest handing back power – which taught me something about the nature of quangos.

Shortly after taking up his role as chairman of the RDC, Vinson suggested there might be some worthwhile lessons to be learned from a visit to the American Small Business Administration – as well as to some of the rural US towns where economic regeneration had been attempted – as a basis to then persuade the UK government to emulate these concepts.

One visit took him to Columbus, Ohio, home of the Cummings Diesel Company – one of the biggest engine makers in the world. Vinson was hugely impressed by the company's philanthropic outlook, which was reflected in its policy of giving 10 per cent of its annual profit to charitable or civic projects. As a result, Columbus possessed some of the finest architectural civic buildings in the world, including several by the great Finnish designer Eero Saarinen, as well as hospitals of a similarly world-class design.

At lunch there, Nigel sat next to the chairman of the company and complimented him on the handsome Henry Moore bronze he had in his quadrangle, remarking that its generous proportions were in perfect harmony with its surroundings. At that point, the waiter came up to the table and said to the chairman, 'Sir, what would you like today?', to which the chairman replied, 'Sir, what would you recommend?' This struck Vinson as a wonderful example of mutual respect reflecting a recognition of their individual tasks.

Vinson was equally impressed by the businessman's response to his compliment about the statue:

Well, it's 12 ft high because big spaces need big statues.
I said to my wife: 'Let's have a Henry Moore.'

To which she said: 'We'll phone him up and ask him about it.'

So I got on to Henry and said: 'What statues have you got?'

And he said: 'Well, I can make you just about anything but tell me the size you want.'

So that afternoon my wife and I got a series of tea chests and I piled them up, one on top of the other. She stood back and looked at the proportions and when the tea chests were stacked four high she said: 'I reckon that's it.'

So I phoned Henry Moore and said to him: 'Henry, it's got to be at least 12 ft high.'

He said 'OK' – and the deal was done.

I am glad you like it.

It confirmed Nigel's view that, given inspirational leadership, regional regeneration can be hugely helped by prosperous and committed local companies: 'Now they are often branches of international businesses – without the same commitment – confirming my opinion that "size is the curse of our time".'

Under Vinson's chairmanship of the RDC, the organisation stepped up its effort to promote private investment, encouraged non-governmental organisations to play a

greater role in the social and economic life of the countryside, and improved and expanded its business advisory
service. In this he was greatly assisted by his deputy and
chairman of the county committees, David Davenport.

More generally, the RDC sought to explain the reali-
ties of country living – and, in particular, what Vinson
described as the 'inescapable effects that distance and
scarcity of population have on economic and social activity' – to a largely urban decision-making elite (who had
little understanding of the problems faced by those living
in rural areas, and sometimes seemed unsympathetic to
their plight). In his 1987–88 chairman's report, Vinson
said that he regarded the task of 'raising national awareness of the rural condition' as being equally important as
the goal of directly boosting jobs and growth.

Using his chairmanship of the Design Council Selection
Committee, he arranged for the Development Commission
to have a joint exhibition at the council's Haymarket show-
rooms. Entitled *Best Made in the Countryside*, the exhibition
was opened by Mrs Thatcher, who left with an armful of
purchases.

Vinson has always maintained that, apart from having
a Poets' Corner in Westminster Abbey, there should be a
Designers' Corner also, to celebrate the huge benefits
such individuals have brought to the economy.

According to Margaret Clark, a senior official at the commission during Vinson's chairmanship, what Nigel brought to the task was a pro-business outlook, an awareness of the part small businesses could play in reviving the rural economy, and a countryman's understanding of the social problems faced by those living in remote areas. She said:

> His approach was sometimes unorthodox and he could be impatient with what he clearly regarded as a public sector approach to problems, but he always listened to colleagues and if we could suggest alternative ways of achieving his objectives, he was ready to heed advice.
>
> And it became clear he was not just concerned with business issues – for example he devised a pilot scheme to provide transport vouchers for those finding it difficult to pay for lengthy visits to relatives in hospital, which turned out to be perfectly feasible and not very expensive, although sadly this was not taken up by government.

Under Vinson's leadership, the commission's successful campaign to remove restrictions on business start-ups in farms led to the creation of thousands of new firms and gave a huge boost to the numbers of self-employed. Nigel told me:

> In making the case more acceptable to the planners, we tried to use the phrase 'craft workshop' wherever possible because it summoned up an idyllic image of a violin-maker plying his ancient craft in a thatched cottage with roses around the door, and it evoked exactly the response we wanted.
>
> In fact, the changes to the law which were brought in opened up the possibility of a much wider range of start-ups than the phrase implies, and gave a great many people the chance to run their own businesses and to have greater control over their lives.

The battle to permit rural businesses the right to place signs directing motorists to their premises attracted opposition from environmental groups – most of which, as Vinson now points out, tend to be based in the city. It is, however, a battle that has had to be refought as environmentalists have continued to seek to influence the decisions of local planning committees. For a small business selling its own products, effective signage can make the difference between success and failure; it is not a trivial matter.

The Redundant Building Grants scheme was very

far-reaching in its effects, providing state funding for the purpose of bringing unused farm buildings back into economic use. Once the scheme had started to demonstrate its success, it was vigorously promoted by the Ministry of Agriculture. Today, clusters of renovated ex-farm buildings, many of which were formerly unused or derelict for decades, have now been turned into workshops, bakeries, art galleries or shops and can be found in every part of rural England. It is estimated that tens of thousands of farm buildings have been brought back into use in this way – not least ARM Ltd, now one of the world's major computer design companies, which started life in such a location.

Nigel Vinson explained the origins of the scheme:

> Having started my own business I realised that finding the right premises at an acceptable cost was as important as finding credit, or even as deciding exactly what to produce. The existence of large numbers of unused farm buildings meant that there was a large potential supply of premises that could be used as workshops or retail outlets and which could be brought into use at a fraction of the cost of new builds (previously the central policy of the commission), and which possessed a quality and charm that would help to attract customers.

It also brought jobs to farms and villages, thereby reducing the need for villagers to travel to towns for work.

Much of Vinson's work involved winning the support of local authorities, as well as the cooperation of those in Westminster and Whitehall. It also meant motivating the regional development committees – whose commitment to rural interest could not be doubted but was not always matched by an understanding of business or government – as they had too readily accepted the bureaucratic obstacles and inertia that impeded their goals.

Lady Dione Digby, who was chairwoman of the Dorset Rural Development Committee, believes that the success of the RDC during Nigel's ten-year chairmanship was due to his motivational skills as well as his powers of persuasion:

> When we left meetings with him we came away thinking we could achieve things we previously thought were beyond us. He motivated us to an extent that I would not have thought possible and gave us confidence that we could make a difference. And we did. Of all the distinguished people I have met in life he impressed me the most, and perhaps has got the least credit for his achievements.

Michael Galsworthy met Nigel Vinson when the former was made an RDC commissioner in 1983:

> My first impression was of a man with a sharp face, sharp nose and a sharp mind. He listened to everyone, regardless of seniority and status, demonstrated a clear strategy for bringing about the renaissance of the English countryside and had an equally clear view about how to achieve what he wanted. He had the aura of a man who is capable of getting things done.

Galsworthy, who farms in Cornwall (and subsequently became a Vice Lord-Lieutenant of the county), was clearly impressed by Vinson's business acumen too, which he believes distinguished him from others who shared the desire to stem the rural economic decline:

> I would say that the Redundant Farm Building Plan, which emerged from the commission under Nigel's chairmanship and which brought back into economic use disused barns and other farm buildings, was the most effective use of public money I know of. It resulted in the creation of a huge number of new small enterprises.

Vinson's methods, which reflected an innate dislike of red tape and bureaucratic inefficiency, were not always conventional. When a decision over where to site a sewage outfall pipe in Cornwall had been delayed for more than a year, he travelled there to address the local authorities and the regional water agency, pointing out the damage being done to the region's economic prospects as a result of the delay.

Lady Mary Holborow, a member of the Cornish Rural Development Committee as well as the local water authority, recalls:

> There had been a great deal of delay and local squabbling. But Nigel came down to read us the riot act. He pointed to the harm that was being done by the procrastination of the authorities concerned and the pressing need to sort out the problem at the earliest possible moment. He told us that unless a decision was reached very soon he would personally see to it that we did not get another penny from the RDC. I could see the chief executive of the commission, who was present at the meeting, looking distinctly uncomfortable because in fact Nigel had no such powers. But his threat and the controversy which it caused had exactly the desired effect. It completely changed

the climate. Within a matter of weeks a decision was reached and the construction went swiftly ahead.

Nigel Vinson spelled out his vision for the countryside in a speech given shortly after his appointment as commission chairman:

> I visualise an economy where essential things like cars and refrigerators will be mass produced elsewhere, but a great deal of small scale activity, computer planning, holiday booking, the production of tourist and craft goods will be conducted from people's homes – and homes in villages ... In my view, the micro-chip will be no more detrimental to employment opportunities than was the spinning jenny.

And so it has proved.

No comprehensive analysis of the RDC's impact or effectiveness has ever been attempted, and Vinson himself has always been keener to move on to the next challenge than to dwell on past glories. But an impression of the commission can be gained from a description of its activities in just one of its annual reports. The report for 1987–88 listed the following achievements:

- Sponsored *Best Made in the Countryside* exhibition at the Design Centre, opened by Margaret Thatcher.

- Assistance to 336 units through the Redundant Buildings Grant scheme with private finance exceeding public money by more than three to one and jobs created at a cost of £1,102 each (a fraction of the normal Department of Industry cost).

- Measures to increase public sector finance available to small, country-based firms, thereby reducing loans from the commission as a proportion of project costs from 80 per cent to 20 per cent.

- The completion of 177,443 square feet of factory space, bringing the total number of square feet of factory space created to more than 3 million, and the creation of many thousands of jobs in the process.

- The provision of business advice to rural firms with a 19 per cent increase in the number of firms registering with the commission's Business Service, bringing the total number of companies on its books to 39,000 – nearly double the number registered five years earlier.

- Assistance in launching 133 new rural transport schemes.

- Marketing grants for more than 600 rural firms to exhibit their products, enabling them to widen their product rage.

Given the RDC's modest budget – £29 million in 1987–88 – and its minimal workforce, this seems like remarkably good value for public money over one year.

By around 2000, England's rural population had ceased to decline and, between 2001 and 2010, the less sparsely populated areas of the English countryside grew more quickly than other parts of Britain. This is not to attribute such a reversal to just one man's attempt at constructing a countryside life-support machine – lower house prices in rural areas, the growth of self-employment resulting in part from the development of information technology, and other economic and social factors have played their part, of course. But there is no doubt that the changes introduced during Vinson's ten-year chairmanship of the RDC gave thousands of people living in rural areas – the vast majority of whom would not have known Nigel Vinson's name – new opportunities and new hope.

Twenty-five years on, it is interesting to see that his work is now endorsed by the EU through their new Rural Development programme – a central pillar of the Common Agricultural Policy, though, as Nigel would say, 'designed in a hugely over-complicated way' – to recognise and mitigate the inherent problems in rural areas.

The free-market purists among Vinson's friends at the IEA would have baulked at the use of public money for state-sponsored interference in the rural economy, but Nigel's reply would be that the modest sums of public money used were necessary to challenge other government departments, cushion the hard edges of change and help lighten the real hardships he had observed first hand.

Schumpeter's description of the market as 'a creative gale of destruction' might indeed convey an inescapable reality about the free enterprise system. However, it does not follow that those who recognise the market's superiority over other economic systems are obliged to oppose the use of public money in providing a temporary lifeline to those caught up in its destructive wake.

CHAPTER 7

Country living

IN AUGUST 1975, Nigel and Vonnie moved to Northumberland, a county whose peace and tranquillity impressed Nigel during his bachelor days. He had first gone there with a girlfriend called Kirsten, whose brother was learning to farm. 'I had a marvellous time and we remained good friends, but I fell in love with the Cheviots, not the girl!' he said later.

Following the birth of Bettina – the eldest of Nigel's three daughters – in July 1974, Nigel decided that

Northumberland was where he would like to raise his new family and farm. He took Vonnie northwards and asked whether she thought she could settle in Northumberland. Yvonne, the daughter of Danish parents, surveyed the rolling countryside stretched out before her and replied: 'I should think so. My ancestors conquered it 2,000 years ago!'

Nigel bought the Roddam Estate – 5 miles south west of the market town of Wooler at the foot of the Cheviots in the northern half of the county – after seeing an advertisement for it in *Country Life*. The estate consisted of: Roddam Hall, an imposing if not elegant stone-built three-storey Georgian house that dates from 1782 (it is listed as a building of historic interest); three farms; two farmhouses; four cottages; and 1,200 acres of farmland. The sale, which was by private treaty, also included an adjoining farm known as Roddam Rigg, four modernised cottages and farm buildings, and a further 456 acres.

The details of sale stated: 'This estate is of considerable charm and offers a unique opportunity to purchase a well laid-out sporting and agricultural investment. Hunting is in the West Percy country – there are five well-known packs in the district.' The sale also included the Roddam Burn, which provided fishing for brown trout.

This beautiful estate on the edge of a national park was to

Nigel – the born countryman – a dream come true and also offered him ample opportunities to shoot, hunt and fish.

The house itself, although surrounded by ornamental hardwoods and with commanding views to the south, could hardly be called beautiful. It was described as 'imposing' in the estate agent's details of sale; its new owner called it 'gaunt'.

Before the sale, Nigel had visualised the house being greatly improved by the removal of the top storey (where, in earlier times, servants had lived). With the help of Tom Bird, an architect and ex-Rifle Brigade staff officer, Nigel developed plans to lop off the top storey and achieve a building of greater simplicity and proportion. These plans, however, attracted suspicion and initial hostility from the Georgian Society, a pressure group that seeks to preserve Georgian buildings, parks and gardens, and campaigns against their neglect, maltreatment or destruction. Today, local authorities have a statutory obligation to consult the group when considering plans to modify listed Georgian buildings. Though it did not possess such powers at the time, the group was still influential and Nigel tried to convince its committee that the changes he was making would enhance and beautify the old house, not damage it.

He set out to win the group over to his way of thinking with customary determination. A series of letters and drawings, together with invitations to visit, followed. Exchanges between Nigel and the group lasted for two years and continued even after the changes to the house had been completed. Eventually, without admitting that it had been wrong, the group withdrew its formal criticism on the grounds it had decided 'that this was a case where compromise was justified if the building was to survive'.

A letter from the group's secretary to Nigel in October 1976 reported that, after three of its members had visited the house, 'the committee shared their delight that [he] had saved this fine building from total dereliction and [was] now so obviously enjoying living in it'. The letter continued: 'You have obviously spent an enormous amount of time and trouble, as well as money, on carrying out the proposals to a very high standard and the committee wishes to convey its congratulations to all concerned.' Finally, the letter concluded with an invitation to Nigel to join the group – a clear indication that he had won the argument.

In addition to lopping off the top storey, Nigel restored each of Roddam's many rooms and restocked the gardens, bringing his asparagus beds from Upton Grey in a trailer. He also threw himself into the task of modernising the farm. For example, he re-routed the road that ran through the courtyard of Roddam Hall by moving it 100 yards north, and, as such, it became wider and safer, thus obtaining the blessing of the planning authority. He also carried out endless repairs to fences and hedgerows. A stone arch, which had stood just outside Plastic Coatings in Friary Square, Guildford (a farewell gift from his former employees at the company), was moved to a nearby hill, where it served not only as a seat, but as a reminder of the business success on which Nigel's good fortune was based.

Later, he was to design an indoor swimming pool with removable staging strong enough to be used as a dance floor for parties – an entirely original idea that turned out to be hugely popular with his daughters. It proved equally popular with the members of the local Womens' Institute, who used it for their functions – probably without realising they were sitting above 6 ft of water.

Roddam provided the perfect setting to display the Vinsons' expanding collection of twentieth-century paintings and *objets d'art*. Among these are works by Augustus John, Gwen John, Alfred Munnings, Ann Redpath and William Nicholson, as well as the nineteenth-century artist Alma-Tadema – all chosen because Nigel was immediately attracted to them, rather than seeing them as investments. He continues to gain considerable enjoyment from painting himself, although his own description of his talents – 'pretty useless, really' – is somewhat on the harsh side.

Nigel's discerning and knowledgeable eye for antiquities enhanced Roddam with Etruscan vases, a Ming Buddha and – his great love – English eighteenth-century walnut furniture. His passion for fine craftsmanship resulted in the purchase of numerous examples of *pietra dura*, a sixteenth-century Armenian icon of a seraphim and the commissioning of a large tapestry of tulips by Elizabeth Blackadder, woven by the Dovecot Tapestry Studio in Edinburgh.

Modern craftworks include one of Elizabeth Frink's bronze aviators and a remarkable set of birds carved in driftwood by Guy Taplin, which continues to claim pride of place on Nigel's desk (he describes it as 'so modern but timeless').

Soon after moving to Northumberland, Nigel and Vonnie decided to follow a traditional Danish custom that requires the bride to bring twelve silver plates to her new household. Leo Wyatt, then reckoned to be the country's finest engraver, was commissioned to inscribe the plates with sayings – repeated below – expressing the truths and values by which the couple have tried to live their lives. The decision was typical of the Vinsons in that it combined a habit of reflecting on, and recording, what is important in life with a love of fine craftsmanship. The original drawings are now with the Ashmolean Museum.

By deeds not words shall ye be judged.

Count your blessings.

Truth and beauty are indivisible.

Keep your friendships in good repair.

Trust all men until you have cause not to.

Intuition is reason in a hurry.

Eyes are the windows of the soul.

In wilderness is the preservation of man.

Truth is more important than consequence.

Unto thine own self be true.

Do as you would be done by.

Freedom of choice is where freedom begins.

Having settled at Roddam, Nigel purchased the neighbouring Hetton Farm Estates, comprising 3,300 acres and
forty-two farm dwellings, for the remarkably modest sum
of £222,000. Although a benign employer, the Co-op – the
estates' previous owner – had been a poor farmer: the farm
was badly organised and equipped, run-down and losing

money. Over the next thirty years, Vinson re-invested any surplus income – and more on top – in rebuilding, re-draining
and constructing new roads, adhering as closely as he could
to the old farming tradition: 'Live as if you would die tomorrow, farm as if you would live forever.' He certainly left the
farms in an infinitely better condition than he found them.

Vinson was now one of the biggest farmers in Northumberland, combining his farming with his directorship of
the CPS, as well as, for some of the time, his work as the
honorary director of the Queen's Silver Jubilee Appeal
and his directorships of other companies, which required
a weekly commute to London.

Northumberland is one of Britain's most conservative
counties, and some locals clearly did not know quite what to
make of this hugely energetic entrepreneur. He had arrived
suddenly in their midst, then immediately thrown himself
into the task of making radical changes to a Georgian property that had not undergone changes for centuries; he had
friends in high places in the government, but he also loved
farming, field sports and the countryside.

Tony Glenton, whose children attended the same preparatory school as Nigel's daughters (and who was later to
act as Nigel's accountant), said: 'For many people, Nigel,
with his well-informed quick mind, was a constant source
of wonderment.'

Nonie, the youngest of the Vinsons' three daughters (who may have been more aware of the attitude aroused by her dynamic father than Nigel himself), said: 'Daddy just about got away with it!'

Nigel, the locals noted, did not suffer fools gladly, but he did share their interest in the topics such as horses and field sports. However, he also seemed to dislike small talk and gossip, preferring to talk about politics, economics, farming or the arts. It was rumoured that he and his wife liked poetry, and that he even wrote the stuff! Although, to his credit, it was recognised that he was quick to support local charities, made a kind and considerate employer, and, shortly after his arrival, became a highly conscientious church warden at St Michael and All Angels in the neighbouring village of Ilderton.

Indeed, church attendance became an established and important feature of the Vinsons' family life. Nigel does not believe in the transcendental aspects of Christianity, or a literal interpretation of the Bible, but he seeks to live his life according to the Christian ethic and he greatly values the sense of community and social cohesion that the Church can provide. He also, as previously mentioned, wants to give thanks for the miracle of existence; in his view, science remains unable to explain the origin of the universe.

After many years of reflection, Nigel came to recognise

that the roots of modern democracy lie in Christian belief, since individuals are ultimately responsible to God, not the state. In *Take Upon Retiring*, the anthology he published in later life, Nigel wrote:

> It has taken me a lifetime to realise that Christianity is the basis of democracy ... Unlike other religions where religion is effectively the state, Christians are responsible for their own morality and at communion break bread with their neighbour signifying that they are all equal in the eyes of God. By putting the individual above the state then, by implication, it is the task of the state to serve a society composed of individuals.

These were not matters that were high up the agenda in the little parish of St Michael and All Angels. But the acceptance of the Vinsons by the small community in which they had chosen to live was assisted by Nigel's practical help in keeping the church in good repair and his enthusiastic support for local good causes. It also helped that Vonnie joined the roster of ladies who shared the tasks of cleaning the church and decorating it with flowers, as well as becoming an active member of the WI. She resumed her work as a speech therapist on a one-day-a-week basis at Morpeth, and then served as a magistrate at Berwick-upon-Tweed, where she acquired a reputation for being both firm and kind.

For his part, Nigel seems not to have noticed the wonderment and possible envy that his lifestyle may have caused, telling London friends that he felt entirely at home in his adopted county and much admired the straightforward values of the local Geordies. He was touched and moved when invited to become a Deputy Lieutenant of the county – a rare honour for someone born outside it. Addressing a local branch of the WI as chairman of the RDC, he told those assembled: 'I may have been born in the south, but I got here as quickly as I could!'

Nigel is not a fatalistic man but he has often been fascinated by the role of seemingly inexplicable coincidences. One such coincidence concerned an 1820 cut-diamond necklace, which he bought at Christie's in 1970 with the aim of accumulating a few pieces of jewellery in preparation for the days when, at long last, he would find a woman he wanted to marry.

In the late 1970s, men still changed for dinner and ladies wore decoration. When Nigel married and later moved to Northumberland, Vonnie subsequently wore the necklace when they dined out with neighbours. At one dinner, Lieutenant General Sir George Collingwood, whose family had owned the Northumberland estate of Lilburn for hundreds of years, commented that the necklace bore a remarkable resemblance to the one his mother used to wear.

'I remember it distinctly because the maid once stole the clasp, and we had to have it replaced with a fake,' he remarked.

Vonnie replied, 'Oh, that *is* a coincidence because this one has a rather strange clasp.'

She then removed the necklace to show it to Collingwood, who was sure that he had seen it before – and, indeed, he had. When Nigel subsequently checked the Christie's inventory it read: 'Property of the Collingwood family'.

Thus, an item of jewellery bought by Nigel before he had any connection with Northumberland, had somehow returned to a household that had not only entertained the Collingwoods regularly through the years, but had also seen the occupants of Lilburn and Roddam intermarry on numerous occasions. Nigel's younger daughters, Rowena and Nonie, subsequently used the necklace as a headpiece at their weddings.

Nigel's and Vonnie's entertaining was often based around shooting parties, comprising friends from the south as well as newfound country neighbours. Nigel appears to have been especially adept at breaking down barriers and putting his guests at ease. When Christopher Ward, the former editor of the *Daily Express* and a relative newcomer to field sports at that time, brought down a hen pheasant, Nigel's keeper, somewhat exceeding his authority, yelled: 'That's a f***ing hen!' To mitigate any embarrassment his guest might feel as a result of this breach of shooting etiquette, Nigel, who normally does not swear, responded: 'Yes, and it's a f***ing good shot!'

Nigel set about transforming the Hetton Estate with characteristic vigour, turning a ramshackle loss-making concern into a modern, well-run farm using the most up to date technology. When he was done, approximately half the land was devoted to livestock and the remainder to arable crops.

Nigel's first and most important decision had been to find a farm manager. The job went to Alan Collett, whose passion for farming matched Nigel's own and who remained with the Vinsons for twenty-three years, until his retirement in 1992. With Collett's help, Nigel added two new milking parlours, two new roads to improve communications on the estate, and a workshop, as well as rebuilding most of the old farm buildings and bringing in the latest farm equipment. By the time Collet retired, staff numbers had expanded to twenty-five, including the maintenance team, and the farm output had hugely increased – although profits were almost entirely devoted to making further farm improvements.

Collet said of Nigel:

Almost his first words to me after giving me the job were, 'Farm this land as if it were your own.' It was marvellous to be given that degree of freedom and responsibility. And if I have any regrets it is that I loved the job so much that I devoted more care and time to it than I did to my family.

Once more adopting his policy of walking the ship, which he had followed at Plastic Coatings, Nigel made a point of locating each of the farm staff as they worked in order to talk to them. This followed a Friday morning meeting with his manager to discuss progress and plans, after which the two men would repair to the Percy Arms, a local pub, for lunch. Collet told me:

If one man had a long-face, Nigel would say, 'What's wrong with him?' He would then try to find out what the problem was in order to do something about it. That approach may be a matter of instinct but I think this is one of the secrets of his success in life and business.

Although Bettina had been born at Upton Grey in July 1974, it was at Roddam Hall that she and her two sisters, Rowena, born in April 1977, and Antonia (Nonie), born in April 1979, were raised.

Bettina, who became an administrator for the Alpha Course at Holy Trinity Church Brompton (before marrying and raising four children of her own), recalls an extremely happy childhood in which outdoor activities, especially riding and hunting, predominated:

> The first thing I realised about my father is that he didn't have a job like other people's daddies. Other people's fathers were away at work or there all of the time because we lived in a rural area and they were farmers. Daddy, who was a farmer for only part of the week, arrived on Thursdays and left on Monday evening, but there was no sense of his being an absent father, and in any case we all went away to board at the age of eight. My recollection is that he was there when we needed him to be around, building things to entertain us and finding exciting things for us to do. He played a huge role in the organisation of birthday parties, which invariably took the form of an assault course around the garden and into the fields, climbing up ladders and using straw bales to climb over walls which, looking back I realise was incredibly dangerous, but enormous fun.
>
> As small children there was a sense of anticipation as we waited for Daddy's arrival from London and

there was a farewell ceremony when he left for London on Monday.

School reports were read to us in a solemn way, but I don't believe that he regarded our school careers as being at all important, perhaps because he did not believe that his own achievements had anything remotely to do with what he had done at school. He showed much greater pride in our appearance, in how we reacted to adults and if we took an interest in what was going on in the world than he would by anything we had done at school. Later on when I told him that I had got a 2:1 in Classics at university he said 'Right, darling!' – and that was that!

If we did anything wrong he would tell us immediately and explain why, but he has always been remarkably forgiving.

Although I didn't realise it at the time it was an incredibly privileged background but despite our many advantages we were always taught to treat people equally. 'Equal, but different,' was the lesson that was repeated to us.

At two or three I was placed on a donkey and I have ridden ever since. I went riding with both my parents and we would also hunt together.

He was always very keen on doing something with

each of us, so he would go riding with me, fishing with Rowena, and he would be involved with Nonie in art and design projects.

Later on, I began to realise that what made him unusual was his desire to deal with the problems of other people and of the world at large – whether they were practical, spiritual, or political, and to seek out others who could solve these if he could not do so directly himself.

I am just immensely proud that now, even in his eighties, my father cannot walk on the other side if he sees someone who needs help. But I do not think he would have achieved as much, or would have been as fulfilled without the incredible support of my mother with her great sense of calm and who, more than any-one I know, is entirely without ego.

Nigel's second daughter Rowena, a teacher and mother of two children, particularly recalls her father's inventiveness:

Father was always coming up with new ideas.

At the back of the Roddam Estate there is a small gravel quarry and one day Father spotted a tiny trans-lucent red stone which turned out to be a carnelian agate – a blood stone. This caused much excitement and subsequently Father asked a digger driver to look out for others. His search yielded half a dozen more – perfect for signet rings. Within a couple of months this is exactly what they were turned into – with a ring for each daughter.

Part of the planning condition for the quarry was that it should be reinstated but Father persuaded the planners that it would be more environmentally advantageous to have a lake at the lowest part. So over the next two years a sluice was constructed, and bull-rushes, bog irises, watercress and other pond plants scrounged from neighbours. Within a few years it was quite charming and won a local award for the best Quarry Restitution. Father stocked the lake with trout and built a raft to encourage us to swim in its wonderful spring water while he stood at the other end and fished.

For his sixty-fifth birthday Father gave himself a wood lathe, something he had always longed to have since a teenager. One of his few relaxations at home is to disappear into his workshop where he became a real expert, not least thanks to his thorough under-standing of an electrician's tasks, in the conversion of vases into bedside lamps – which were even weighted at the bottom so that if accidentally hit in the night they would self-correct to the vertical.

More recently his inventiveness discovered that
you can make a wonderful poached egg by breaking it into a breakfast cup and giving it thirty-two
seconds in the microwave. Jane Lovett, a local cook-
ery expert, was so impressed she regularly passes this
tip on to her cooking classes.

Rowena fondly remembers fishing expeditions with her
father. As friends who have enjoyed the experience of being
invited to fish with him will know, Nigel's idea of the sport
does not correspond with the stereotype of a solitary lone
fisherman standing patiently for endless hours in order to
land a fish. Although occasionally interspersed with a break
to read a book or newspaper (or have a nap), for Nigel,
fishing is a high action pursuit expected to yield immediate results.

Rowena recalls:

Fishing with daddy was hilarious. In practice, this
meant standing next to him while he did everything from beginning to end while keeping up a
running commentary. But I learned a great deal and
in fact I came to love fishing and the sense of peace
which it gave my father and which I came to enjoy
myself.

Nonie, his youngest daughter and a mother of three children, weighs in:

> He is a unique combination of strength and compassion. I think he subconsciously encouraged the same in his daughters. The aspiration was to be absolutely feminine and yet capable of killing and skinning a rabbit, plucking game and gutting fish – much like my mother, I suppose.
>
> I recently took our children for a ride through an over-grown wood – under spiky blackthorn, through boggy bits, dodging badgers' setts, up and down steep banks – and turned to my husband and said: 'This is what riding with my father was like! If we so much as grumbled he would say: 'Don't be so b****y wet!'
>
> Both our parents have a real knowledge of the countryside and were always keen to teach us the identification of flowers, trees and birds – though sadly I don't think we always wanted to listen! – but I value that input hugely as an adult, and also the realisation of what they created at Roddam.
>
> Our upbringing there was 'the good life' – almost self-sufficient living off the land; water from a natural spring, milk from a house-cow. We would collect the full pails before breakfast and then grumble that

fresh warm milk made the cereal soggy in minutes! How spoilt! Lamb, beef, rabbit, hare, trout, salmon, partridge, grouse, pheasant, pheasant, more pheasant... On top of that our parents made the most wonderful kitchen garden – the gleaning of which was mummy's delight.

My parents imparted a valuable appreciation of the arts in all of us. I recall being teased by my school friends for being a 'culture vulture' and until then hadn't realised it was anything out of the ordinary. Bearing in mind that we lived in the middle of nowhere, they did an impressive feat in taking us to exhibitions, classical concerts, musical theatre and opera. One Christmas, when I must have been about seven, Daddy announced that as a treat he had bought us a video. Wow! After the Queen's speech and presents we raced to the nursery in great anticipation! The video began, and then our hearts sank … 'How to build a castle. Scene One. The Motte and Bailey'. Only one person was glued to the telly that afternoon; three skirts had made a swift exit!

I remember a particularly special day with my father when he and I took a day trip to the Lake District to see a temporary Lucian Freud exhibition. He put the time aside to enable me to pursue my interest and must have driven over four hours for the sake of a handful of paintings. Always indefatigable.

My mother has a great eye for colour and my father for design, both of which have shaped my chosen career hugely. When they came to visit me in Italy [where she was studying at the Charles Cecil School of Art in Florence] it was like an explosion of appreciation in my parents. A day in Florence best sums up the polymath that is NV.

Talking to neighbours in the small community of Roddam some time in 1995, Nigel realised that, since there were no other Roddams anywhere in the world, the family of Hillary Rodham Clinton must have come from that village, despite the slight difference in the spelling of the names. So Nigel telephoned the American embassy and asked whether they thought she might welcome an invitation to visit the place of her family's origin. Encouraged by the response, he composed the following letter:

Dear Mrs Clinton,

I write from the village of Roddam in Northumberland – and, as there appear to be no other Roddam habitations anywhere in the world, I think perhaps your family may have originated here.

So I send you sincere good wishes from the twelve citizens in the home of your forebears – with the hope that you might give us the pleasure of showing you round should you come over with the President on his next visit to the United Kingdom.

On behalf of our small community,
Lord Vinson of Roddam Dene, LVO, DL

He later received a letter from the White House saying that Mrs Clinton would love to visit Roddam at some point in the future, but, in the meantime, would Nigel and his family like to visit the White House? This was an offer the Vinson family promptly took up, arriving at the White House in a huge stretch limo. The White House helicopter may not subsequently have appeared over Roddam, but, as Mrs Clinton prepares her challenge for the presidency in 2016, the Vinsons remain hopeful that she will recognise the photo opportunity presented by an invitation to visit the picturesque rural home of her forefathers and allow the Vinsons to repay the hospitality they were shown in Washington DC.

THE WHITE HOUSE

August 9, 1995

The Lady Joseph
Sunnyside Farm
32 Calhoun Hill Road
Washington, Connecticut 06793

Dear Lady Joseph:

Thank you for making arrangements through the White House Visitors Office for The Lord Vinson and his family to have a private tour in July. We are honored that they came. The greetings he brought from the village of Roddam were of special meaning for me, since some of my ancestors were from that area.

I appreciate your kind words commending our staff, and Ron Passalaqua in particular, for the outstanding manner in which your request was handled.

With best regards, I am

Sincerely yours,

Hillary Rodham Clinton

After inviting the First Lady Hillary Rodham Clinton to Roddam,

she returned the compliment by inviting the Vinsons to the White House.

Family holidays were often to the Spanish estate the Vinsons had purchased shortly after their marriage. As in the case of the Roddam Estate, Nigel had been persuaded to purchase by the unspoiled beauty of the countryside. They had fallen in love with it when he and Vonnie joined a shooting party outside the ancient fortified town of Montiel in Castilla-La Mancha, which was organised by his friend Tom Gullick, an internationally known ornithologist who had boosted the local economy by bringing the English way of driving partridges to Spain.

Since there was no Spanish equivalent of Knight Frank to assist, Nigel asked Gullick to help find him a suitable property. Having consulted the locals, Tom found exactly what the Vinsons were looking for – a 2,000-acre estate with a small river running through it, two hills rising to about 400 ft, a tumble-down shepherd's cottage and a freshwater spring. They christened it Vinosmena, and planted vines on one small parcel of the land – although, as Nigel ruefully acknowledged, this did more for the wild boar who feasted on them than it did for the production of wine, with only a small quantity of the vines' produce going each year to the local wine cooperative.

Apart from partridge shooting, the chief delight was riding through the unspoiled countryside in the spring. Forty years later, Nigel can still recall one particular four-hour ride during which, without leaving the borders of his own property, he saw four eagle owls, two golden eagles, a wild boar and its piglets, an extremely rare Spanish lynx, hares, rabbits, a 4-foot water snake and an otter in the shade of an unmarked Roman bridge.

Such delights compensated for the problems of running an estate from afar. The farmer Nigel contracted to cultivate the rough areas of grain land, which were needed to encourage the partridges, constantly demanded new machinery. Lightning struck the electricity shortly after Nigel had paid for this to be installed and the keeper's wife grew tired of living 20 miles from the nearest village, so the property was left unprotected as a result.

There were also occasional language problems. At the end of a lunch during which copious amounts of wine had been consumed, Nigel's Spanish keeper arrived to ask what time he would like the horses fetched for his evening ride. Nigel wanted four horses at four o'clock – *cuatro caballos a cuatro* – but, using his modest and newly acquired Spanish vocabulary, he mistakenly asked for *cuatro caballeros a cuatro* – which means four young gentlemen at four o'clock. With a huge smile on his face, the keeper left hotfoot to the village to spread the magnificent tale of the Englishman's strange request. The following day, Spanish women in black dresses turned their children's faces to the wall, wagging crinkled arthritic fingers as the eccentric lord passed by.

Sadly, the pleasure of owning Vinosmena diminished over the years as the local shepherds abandoned horses in favour of quad bikes. The bikes were easier and cheaper to maintain, but this change meant it was no longer possible to hire horses to ride.

Nigel, therefore, decided to sell but, after receiving half the agreed price from the purchaser, a legal battle followed when the new owner challenged the title deeds. After seven years and several court cases, Nigel was assured by his lawyer that their case was watertight and that victory was finally at hand – only for the judge, having checked all the relevant papers, to determine that the case was out of time by one day under the statute of limitations. Despite having lost money on the deal, Nigel has few regrets: in his view, the recollection of rides through the unspoiled countryside of the Sierra, covered in spring flowers and teeming with wildlife, compensates for the loss.

By the late 1990s, Nigel had come to the conclusion that, with no male heir to inherit his house and land, it was time to scale down his farming activities and downsize. Accordingly, in 2002 (in Nigel's seventy-first year), the Hetton Estate was placed on the market. The agent acting on Nigel's behalf described the 400-strong dairy herd as 'the jewel in the crown' of the six-farm estate. The purchaser was a local businessman.

Some way into the deal, Nigel had an intuitive feeling that things were not going well and that he should pull out. On the other hand, he was seventy years old and anxious to get on with the task of redistributing his wealth before he died.

During the sale negotiations, he told the purchaser: 'Obviously I can't dictate what you do with the farm but one thing is central to the deal and that is you should retain my farm manager.' Accordingly, the farm manager was told by the purchaser: 'You can work for me as long as you like.'

Nigel later recalled:

> Despite inner misgivings, I sold in full confidence that all would go ahead as I wished – with my farm manager continuing in his job – but was shocked to learn that the new owner had changed his mind and sacked him within three hours of signing the contract. One of the instances in my life where my trust was ill-founded.

Nigel's only consolation was that most of those dismissed by the new owner, including the farm manager, subsequently found worthwhile jobs.

Nigel told me:

It is more than ten years since all of this occurred. At the time I was mortified that I should have so badly let down those who relied on me, and I continue to be troubled by the distress that the sale caused to those who had shown personal loyalty. Although all of those who were thrown out of their jobs found other work it remains a matter of huge regret.

The sale in 2012 of Roddam Hall and the 1,100 acres of farmland on the Roddam Estate to James Percy, younger brother of the Duke of Northumberland, had happier consequences. Following a classic country house sale of antiques, furniture, paintings and collectables that Vinson and his wife had accumulated over more than three decades, the couple moved just over a mile away to a new, elegant but homely, neo-Georgian stone farmhouse built over the foundations of the old Roddam Rigg farmhouse.

He told me: 'I had always wanted to build a "Gentleman's Residence" – as an estate agent might put it – since reading *The House That Berry Built* by Dornford Yates when I was a boy. My dream came true at Roddam Rigg.'

Assisted by a local draughtsman Ian Mark, but without the services of an architect, Nigel drew up the plans himself – a remarkable achievement for a man without architectural qualifications of any kind who was then in his eightieth year (even if he did have a lifelong passion for good design). The house, which overlooks miles of unspoiled countryside, is smaller than Roddam Hall, but large enough to accommodate Nigel and Vonnie's nine grandchildren during school holidays, as well as a steady stream of London visitors, their most prized paintings and their *objets d'art.*

Several friends have lamented the fact that, because it was not designed by an architect, the house is not eligible for architectural design competitions, in which it might very well have achieved high honours – not least for its pleasing stonework, elegant hipped roof, grey-green slating, traditional sash windows and beautiful interior arched stairway.

As Nigel said: 'It has proved to be such a successful home – both charming and practical.' He was delighted when the Newcastle Architectural Society organised a visit in order for their members to view a fine example of a modern country house. Possibly the best compliment was the immediate adoption of the house by five pairs of nesting house martins – thought to be a lucky omen!

CHAPTER 8

Capitalism for all

MARGARET THATCHER'S VISION of a property-owning democracy made Britain more middle class, destroying the rationale of left-wing theorists and trade union militants who believed that class conflict was inevitable. The wider ownership of wealth meant not only that the interests of bosses and workers were seen to be more closely aligned, but also that the benefits of a market economy were more widely understood. By the time Thatcher left office, more people owned shares than belonged to trade unions, and the number of those owning their own homes had rocketed. Moreover, the role of the entrepreneur – which Keith Joseph had feared would never be appreciated in this country – came to be recognised as the essential catalyst of wealth creation.

Margaret Thatcher's reputation as the greatest peace-time Conservative Prime Minister of the twentieth century is largely a consequence of this transformation, but credit also belongs to two groups of individuals. The first consists of those who made possible the intellectual sea change necessary to bring about the transformation (many of whom are described in a previous chapter), and the second comprises those who shaped the policies through which it was achieved. The two groups are not mutually exclusive; Nigel Vinson deserves credit for having played a significant role in both of these processes.

As a young entrepreneur, Vinson had come to realise that the best way to get people to embrace the market economy was to give them a stake in its success – a principle he had put into practice in his own company.

Vinson wanted Conservative governments to promote 'popular capitalism' not just 'capitalism', which, in his view, left people with the idea that the market was merely the interaction of impersonal forces. Similarly, he favoured the term 'social market economy', rather than just the 'market economy', since the former drew attention to the role of the market order in providing public services and buttressing liberty, not just producing consumer goods.

At the heart of Vinson's political philosophy was the recognition that economic power should be more widely diffused. This may have been refined as a result of his contact with the Conservative intellectuals of the Bow Group, the IEA and the CPS – but Vinson has remained the same in terms of fundamentals throughout his life. It seemed obvious to him that individuals had more opportunities – and could therefore be said to be more *free* – if they possessed material wealth. His views on this matter brought him into conflict with his friends at the IEA and the CPS who adhered to the classical liberal position that freedom is essentially a negative concept and merely implies the absence of external constraint. Keith Joseph liked to illustrate the point by arguing that, under Vinson's logic, it followed that a well-fed prisoner would be freer than a carefree but penniless vagabond. The matter was not entirely academic since, at that time, left-wing ideologues argued that economic redistribution by the state could expand the area of human liberty.

Vinson was not persuaded by Joseph's arguments, though, and sent him a memo in which Nigel asserted:

'Freedom begins when you have £1,000 in the bank.' Vinson says that, if he were writing the same memo today he would give freedom's starting point as £10,000 – or the approximate equivalent of six months' average salary – but that he has not changed his view. To Vinson, it seems only a matter of common sense that wealth extends opportunities, and, when common sense (with which Vinson is very amply endowed) collides with doctrinal purity, he unhesitatingly chooses the former. His coat of arms bears the words: 'No freedom without choice'.

However, this philosophical disagreement between the two men made very little difference in policy terms. Both believed in the restorative power of capitalism to achieve national renewal and both also believed, quite passionately, that wealth should be spread more evenly. In several speeches, Joseph repeated the idea that Britain needed more millionaires – perhaps he entertained the optimistic assumption that, if this were to happen (as it later did, following the supply-side reforms of the '80s), a greater number of them would turn out to be as generous and public-spirited as Vinson.

Although they differed on a number of matters, Joseph and Vinson agreed about the central importance of creating multiple sources of patronage – 'the very yeast and stimulus of a civilised society', to use Joseph's words.

Along with others at the CPS, Vinson contributed ideas and suggestions to a speech that was to be repeated by Joseph at more than 100 universities during the period between 1975 and 1979. In this speech, Joseph put forth the moral as well as material case for market order, and dwelt at length on the fundamental importance of the link between economic and political freedom.

During earlier decades, Tories had customarily argued that socialist ideas might be noble in theory but did not work in practice. Joseph now exposed those ideas directly to withering intellectual scrutiny.

The speech drew hostile responses at several campuses, but it also packed lecture halls. For the first time, a senior Conservative politician, in advancing the case for capitalism, was prepared to lay claim to the intellectual and moral high ground in a way that combined passion with rigour and admitted past errors, but did not talk down to the young audiences it addressed.

Pointing at the link between economic, political and spiritual freedom, Joseph asked his audience:

'Who is the person who, in the last 150 years, has most changed the world?'

At this point, at least one person would reply with exactly the answer Joseph wanted: 'Karl Marx'.

Joseph continued:

You have guessed. Can there be any doubt. It *is* Karl
Marx. Now Karl Marx was expelled from Germany,
he was expelled from France, he was expelled from
Holland. In each case as a revolutionary. He came to
this country as a penniless political refugee – and for
twenty-five years worked away in the British Museum
Reading Room. He wrote *Das Capital* and launched
the Communist Manifesto.

What did he live on? Did he live on supplementary
benefit? Was he a writer in residence at a British university? Did he get a pension from the government?
No, he was supported by one of the large owners of
wealth in a free society. He was supported for twenty-
five years by a Manchester business family called
Engels!

Joseph pointed out that, in contrast to societies with command economies, free economies contained numerous
individuals, companies, charities and foundations to whom
the writer, artist, inventor, reformer and social critic could
appeal for support.

In a command society such individuals must go before
officials. Supposing you want to start a magazine. You
must put your case to officials. They will ask about its

editorial policy. Suppose you say that the purpose will be to expose hypocrisy and corruption among the ruling class and when you are asked for the name of the publication you wish to start, you reply: 'Well, I was thinking of calling it *Private Eye*.' Do you imagine, even for a moment, that the funds would be forthcoming?

This was the kind of argument that undergraduates had not heard before, and it helped shape the attitudes of a new generation of Conservative activists, as well as dumbfounding and outraging left-wingers.

Recognising the importance of influencing politicians of the future, Vinson was an enthusiastic backer of the CPS's activities targeted at young people. These included weekend seminars at which Conservative academics, journalists and politicians put forward both the material *and* moral case for the market to invited audiences of student leaders. For more than a decade, Vinson helped fund the International Society of the Open University – a week-long summer school held at a Cambridge college with broadly similar aims that ran with the help of Dr Madsen Pirie and Dr Eamonn Butler of the Adam Smith Institute. Vinson also helped fund the Alternative Bookshop in Floral Street, which specialised in Conservative and libertarian texts. Again, this endeavour had the aim of challenging the predominantly left-wing intellectual climate that existed in Britain in the 1970s, and, in particular, the socialist influence on the younger generation of undergraduates.

Such was the extent of Nigel Vinson's commitment to the goal of diffusing economic power that he was not slow to criticise the Thatcher government when he thought it was moving with insufficient resolve to achieve this – even the Prime Minister herself.

In April 1982, at the annual meeting of the CPS (where the chairmen of the think tank's study groups gave personal progress reports to the Prime Minister), Vinson, chairman of the centre's Personal Capital Formation Group,[6] rebuked Mrs Thatcher for giving the impression that the defeat of inflation through monetary measures was an end in itself, and for not doing enough to spread the benefits of economic growth more widely. He said:

> Monetary theories are difficult to grasp but the personal ownership of wealth, in all its forms, is something people can readily understand and find instantly attractive. But this historic message is simply not getting through. We know the party believes in wider ownership and the dissemination of wealth

---

6 Later renamed the Wider Ownership Study Group.

– of course we do – but we see no attempt to orches-
trate this philosophical commitment.

Three years later, in a CPS paper co-written with his close
friend Philip Chappell, the authors advocated the introduction of Personal Investment Pools – later to be renamed
Pension Equity Plans. In it, Nigel wrote: 'A government
committed to the encouragement of enterprise and the
principle of wider ownership might have been expected
to introduce wider reforms … People desire ownership,
enjoy ownership and will vote for ownership.'

Nevertheless, despite Nigel Vinson's frustration at the
pace and scope of change, a huge amount was achieved. As
a result of Thatcher's Right to Buy scheme, introduced as
part of the 1980 Housing Act, the number of home owners rocketed from 9.68 million to 12.782 million in 1990
(the year Thatcher left office), and the figure continued to
grow until it peaked at 14.791 million in 2005. For the first
time, secure tenants of councils and housing associations
were given the legal right to buy their own home. The sale
price of a council house was based on its market valuation
but also included a generous discount based on the length
of the tenant's occupancy as a means of encouraging the
take-up. Proceeds of the sale were paid to local authorities
who were restricted to using the money to pay off debt.

The reform, which lifted millions of working people into the middle class, was popular with those who took advantage of the legislation, but bitterly opposed by the Labour Party, who pledged to repeal the legislation in their 1983 election manifesto. Recognising the political difficulties they would encounter by continuing to oppose the scheme, Labour finally dropped their pledge, although they did reduce the size of the discount available to some would-be buyers when they returned to office in 1997.

Mrs Thatcher subsequently admitted that, at first, her middle-class prejudices made her wary of selling off council houses at much reduced prices. She had feared the idea would offend existing home owners who had struggled to buy homes in the private sector, but she also grasped the wider economic and social significance of the reform. In her eyes, owning your own home was a clear sign of the middle-class values she wished to propagate.

At the same time as the Right to Buy scheme was being established, changes to the banking sector – including the lifting of exchange controls and the opening of capital markets – created a much more competitive mortgage market, providing loans to many people who would previously not have been able to afford them (a trend that may have been taken too far in the past decade).

Largely as a result of wider home ownership, household

wealth in Britain has grown rapidly to £7 trillion for the first time, with average household wealth standing at £255,500 in 2012.

As Richard Cockett noted in *Thinking the Unthinkable*, the impact that the CPS had on micro-economic policy and trade union policy – the two key elements of Mrs Thatcher's programme of radical reform – was vital and substantial, if not matched by its influence on other aspects of the government's work.

Nigel Vinson's direct influence on policy was achieved through the centre's Wider Ownership Group, which he continued to chair after standing down as CPS treasurer. The group – consisting of two other highly successful entrepreneurs (David Cooksey and Brian Kingham), two MPs, a merchant banker and a Conservative trade unionist – produced a stream of well-researched ideas and suggestions on how to diffuse economic power, encourage savings and reform the pension system.

At the annual meeting of the CPS on 1 February 1989, Vinson told those present:

> The philosophy behind the work of the Wider Ownership Group is the belief that the diffusion of economic power is the pre-requisite of a free and open society. The market is the best mechanism for

achieving these but must be seen as a means and not an end in itself...

As Tories, we preach wider ownership and all the benefits that flow from it; in practice we have done too little to tackle the causes that increasingly concentrate power. Fiscal policies favour institutional rather than personal investment. Regulatory requirements, which should have helped the consumer, have made the cost of trading small shareholdings uneconomic. Many financial institutions see no benefit in encouraging wider ownership...

We believe that the gold thread of the party's commitment to personal ownership and individual responsibility should guide all the work done by the centre in other economic and social fields – health, education, privatisation etc. It is one which the electorate wants.

As Cockett also notes, the Wider Share Ownership Group was one of the most successful of all the CPS's study groups, coming up with three major proposals that later became government policy and had an impact on the lives of millions: Personal Pensions; Pension Equity Plans; and the Enterprise Allowance scheme.

In Vinson's words, the point of the third scheme was to

'legitimise moonlighting' and he put his ideas personally to Jim Prior – with whom, almost uniquely for a Thatcherite, he enjoyed good personal relations – when the latter was Minister of Employment. In March 1983, the government finally introduced the scheme and Prior sent a letter of congratulations: 'It has taken a long while to persuade the Treasury to make the enterprise allowance a national scheme – the wheels of government grind slow. It was an idea you hatched in my office and I am delighted it has come to something.'

The scheme gave a guaranteed income of £40 a week to unemployed people who set up their own businesses. It was first announced on 13 November 1981 and piloted between January 1982 and July 1983. It was introduced nationwide in 1983 – against a background of rising unemployment – and subsequently funded 325,000 aspiring entrepreneurs. Those wishing to claim from the scheme were required to provide the first £1,000 out of their own funds and produce a business plan. In some respects, the scheme reflected Vinson's work with Young Enterprise when he was running Plastic Coatings. A similar project – the Back to Work Enterprise scheme – was also launched in Ireland.

Among the diverse list of beneficiaries were: Alan McGee, the founder of Creation Records (a company that enjoyed international success before being bought out by Sony); the founders of *Viz* (an adult comic magazine); and Julian Dunkerton, the head of Superdry (a men's clothing company that opened its first store in Covent Garden in 2004 and floated on the London Stock Exchange in March 2010). Dunkerton appeared on the *Sunday Times* Rich List 2010 and is said to be worth an estimated £180 million.

Another beneficiary was Tracey Emin, who used the cash to set up a shop in Bethnal Green in 1993 that sold T-shirts and ashtrays with the photo of another struggling artist – by the name of Damien Hirst – on them.

Critics of the scheme pointed to the fact that one in six of the start-up businesses failed within the first year. But, as those who signed up to the scheme discovered, the market entails a continuous process of trial and error. In the normal run of things, though, five out of six business start-ups fail at an early stage; the Enterprise Allowance scheme may therefore be considered a significant success. Even those who tried and failed are likely to have gained valuable experience of which they could subsequently take advantage, and several are known to have recovered their confidence sufficiently to launch start-ups at a later date.

After home ownership, Vinson and his paper co-author Chappell saw that the next best step in creating a capital-owning democracy was to re-attribute the wealth in pension funds to the ultimate beneficiaries – pensioners. They compared this to the work of Henry VIII, whose 'dissolution of the monasteries' preceded (by some 400 years) their desire to see the 'dissolution of the institutions' through lessening their direct ownership of pension wealth.

The hard intellectual labour behind Norman Fowler's pension reforms of 1985 had been carried out by the CPS Wider Ownership Group, and, in particular, by Vinson and Chappell. A succinct six-page memorandum prepared by the group, entitled 'Personal and Portable Pensions – For All', had been published two years earlier (in April 1983) and was specific about what needed to be done:

> There should be a fundamental review of pension legislation to remove the penalty on changing jobs, to aid mobility and to link individuals more closely with the wealth represented by their pension fund. To these ends pensions should, as far as possible, become personal and portable, identifiable by the employee and attributable to him.

Not surprisingly, Nigel Vinson's favourite aphorism, attributed to Aristotle, is: 'Where no one owneth, no one careth.'

The Vinson–Chappell proposals reflected a strong belief that existing arrangements unfairly penalised those who changed jobs. Vinson and his group wanted to remove

the 'golden handcuffs' that discouraged labour mobility, in order to give employees a much greater say. Nigel
continued:

> There is currently deep concern at the grave injustices
> inflicted on those who change jobs – the so called
> 'early leaver'. This injustice is indefensible; what is
> more it leads to ossification of employment patterns
> and harms the whole nation by inhibiting enterprise.
>
> The problem arises from the traditional atti-
> tude (increasingly questioned) that pensions are an
> optional gift from the employer and thus the employee
> should not be entitled to more than the return of his
> or her contributions, when leaving. Indeed, under-
> standably, many employers have regarded the pension
> fund as a means of retaining and rewarding long-ser-
> vice employees.

The Vinson–Chappell proposals possessed two cardinal
virtues. The first was that they faced up to an unpalat-
able but unavoidable truth, which many had chosen to
ignore: namely, that pension benefits were an unquanti-
fiable burden of cost on a company's finances at a time
when people were living longer – a situation that could
not be sustained indefinitely. Secondly, they came up with

a detailed plan to move to personal pensions with defined contributions jointly funded by employer and employee, which indeed has happened. Vinson and Chappell also took heart from the fact that their proposals fully reflected the wider ownership philosophy both men had sought to promote throughout their lives.

When the CBI's group on wider ownership, of which Vinson was a member, produced proposals that, in his view, did not go far enough, he produced a minority report. He argued that few people had enough money to save for their pension and make additional savings. The best approach was to give them access, within reasonable limits, to their own individual pensions, which would, in future, be attributed to them, although held collectively – 'thereby turning nobody's money into somebody's money'.

Nevertheless, their proposals on pensions, especially those that enabled employees to take their pension from one job to another, were fiercely resisted at the time by the pensions industry. Addressing a National Association of Pension Funds meeting, Vinson reminded them: 'All pensions are ultimately paid out of the GNP – occupational pensions are merely an inter-generational lien on that wealth, which would be better owned by the pensioner not an institution.'

According to Norman Fowler:

The industry was horrified. They saw this as a direct threat to their final salary schemes. Reform was one thing. But this was revolution. They were right. Company pension schemes were the golden handcuffs which chained staff to a company. Portable pensions could give people more freedom and end the penalty on changing jobs.

Vinson's and Chappell's paper won numerous converts in the media, including writers on the *Daily Telegraph*, the *Financial Times*, the *Investor's Chronicle*, the City pages of the London *Evening Standard* and *The Times*, which described their arguments as 'compelling' and urged the government to give them immediate and serious consideration. Even *The Guardian*, which could normally be relied upon to criticise CPS publications, conceded: 'It would be wrong lightly to dismiss Mr Vinson's arguments.' Wrong, *lightly* to dismiss them, indeed – but *The Guardian* then went on to point to other administrative factors that discouraged the introduction of the arguments anyway.

That the proposals went through relatively painlessly compared to some other Thatcherite reforms was due to the fact that the intellectual heavy lifting had been painstakingly performed by Vinson and Chappell. Moreover, to quote Christopher Fildes (the doyen of Fleet Street's City commentators), the new Social Services Secretary Norman Fowler had taken up the idea of pension reform 'with a fair wind blowing behind him, at gale force, from Downing Street'.

Although the two were on Christian-name terms, Nigel Vinson and Margaret Thatcher did not enjoy a close personal relationship. The fact that Mrs Thatcher threw her weight behind proposals affecting the lives of millions of voters had as much to do with trusting Nigel's judgement as it did with the proposals bearing the imprimatur of the CPS, which she regarded as a clear indication of ideological soundness. Both before and after the publication of 'Personal and Portable Pensions – For All', Vinson and Chappell had prepared their opinion for the reforms through a stream of articles and letters in the media, which could not be dismissed as the work of those with a vested interest in the subject.

Pension arrangements were extremely complicated and considered by many to be an uninteresting, even boring, field for intellectual inquiry. The work done by the group, especially Vinson and his deputy chairman Chappell, was necessarily painstaking and involved considerable application over several years. Neither man had anything to gain personally from the reform of pensions and neither was a pension expert by background, although they both became such through a shared conviction that the existing pension system was deeply unfair, rested on questionable assumptions, seriously discouraged enterprise and was not sustainable in the long term. Both believed that reform was necessary if people were to understand how freedom and prosperity depended on popular capitalism.

In a letter to *The Times* on 28 September 1983, Vinson and Chappell wrote:

> Overall our proposals give the chance to be more fair to those who in our increasingly labour mobile times, might wish to have the option – the freedom to choose – to take their pensions with them, as the self-employed can. What is more, they encourage the dissemination of ownership, that essential condition for a free and responsible society.

In their campaign to make pensions transportable and to give employees greater control of their pension entitlements, they found a robust ally in Frank Field, the principled and independent-minded Labour MP for Birkenhead, who had reached similar views about the need for pension reform. Field was to become a good personal friend of Nigel Vinson; within Westminster, friendships rarely cross party boundaries, but each recognised in the other a readiness to put the national interest before their parties' and not to allow considerations of personal interest to discourage them from doing so.

Subsequently, Vinson and Field signed a joint letter urging Alistair Darling to encourage pension investment in infrastructure funds and this was repeated to the current Chancellor George Osborne. The letters went unanswered but the concept is now widely accepted and adopted.

Field has later said of Vinson:

> Leaving aside his record as an entrepreneur and his contributions to two organisations which changed the political direction of this country, what I admire most about Nigel is his spirit. You know that if Britain was invaded tomorrow Nigel would be there leading the fight to repel the invaders.

When the reforms were introduced, Vinson and Chappell received very little by way of recognition. Norman Fowler, in describing the passage of the reforms through Parliament in his autobiography, does not even mention their names. It was left to Christopher Fildes, writing in his column in *The Spectator*, to reveal the origins of the changes, grasp their full significance and explain the importance of happenstance in the making of history:

Two summers ago, Nigel Vinson, the inventor, bumped into Philip Chappell, the merchant banker, walking across Green Park. This week that bump detonated an explosion under £90 billion of managed money that will transform countless working lives and the retirements that should follow them. Mr Vinson is a man with a vision. He believes that for a free market to work, as many people as possible must have a direct stake in it. Selling council houses was a major step in that direction, and a major winner, too. 'What could follow it?' said the banker and the inventor to each other that day in the park. People's pension rights, under the state and employers' schemes, are worth as much as the nation's housing stock, public and private. For most people, their pension rights vie with their houses as their most valuable asset. Yet how few of those people have any sense of owning those pension rights, let alone of owning their pension funds' investments? How few know what those rights are, have any control of them, any choice at all? Said the inventor and the banker: 'Let's have a go.'

The introduction of personal pensions was initially marred by the pension industry's mis-selling and erroneous advice, encouraging many older workers to transfer when their

best interests would have been served by seeing their con-
tracts out until retirement.

Then followed their next idea: PEPs were introduced
in 1987 by the then Chancellor Nigel Lawson with the
idea of encouraging people to buy company shares as
well as promoting the goal of popular capitalism Vinson
had long advocated. This scheme, which enabled investors to enjoy the benefits of stock market profits free of
income tax and capital gains, was initially limited to a
narrow range of possible investments, but it later widened
to include unit trusts, investment trusts and corporate
bonds.

The scheme had the support of a number of Tory MPs
and free enterprise groups, all of which deserve credit for
its subsequent success. But few championed its goal with
such determination as Vinson, whose publication 'Owners All: A Proposal for Personal Investment Pools (PIPs)',
co-authored with Chappell again, set out the underlying
political philosophy of the scheme, as well as describing in
detail the existing barriers to the wider diffusion of ownership. Vinson and Chappell set out the principal aims of
the scheme with clarity and rigour:

> Few human aspirations are stronger than owner-
> ship. Nor will it be denied that ownership can confer

independence and dignity. But it must be personal. Widely diffused, it serves as one of the principal foundations of an open society...

Only if individuals participate directly in the creation of wealth can they understand the benefits which it brings to society at large. Ownership at second hand, whether through institutions or the state, is a sorry substitute. Institutionalised capitalism, because of its concentration of power and diminishment of individual enterprise, is just as much a betrayal of the open society as socialism itself. Diffusion of resources is a cornerstone of freedom, since it builds choice by the customer into the fabric of society ... Even if wider personal ownership will not of itself solve our economic difficulties, it is vital that it should be, and should be seen to be, part of the basic framework of a wealth creating society.

Socialists argue that the central ownership of wealth makes for impartiality and equality. Others take a feudal view – individuals cannot be trusted to make their own decisions and must be protected from their follies: this leads to a cryptic form of socialism, masquerading as benevolent paternalism. Fortunately, the voices of individuals, eager and able to reassert their right to personal ownership, are heard throughout history. Diffusion of ownership does more than diffuse wealth. It spreads initiative, spreads the power of patronage, and strengthens the foundations of a free and open society.

At first, the take-up of PEPs was modest, with 270,000 people acquiring them in the first year, and the timing was less than fortuitous since the 1987 stock market crash came just a year after the scheme's introduction. Despite this, more than three million people today have either a PEP or a stock market ISA (as the schemes were rebranded in 1999). Following the introduction of ISAs on 6 April 1999 by the New Labour government, no new contributions could be made to PEPs, although existing funds retained their tax privileges. As one investment analyst has pointed out, anyone who invested in the full PEP allowance each year and the full ISA allowance in subsequent years would be sitting on an investment of £500,000. Vinson's dream of a society in which wealth was more widely dispersed has become a reality, although he is saddened that the progress achieved during the 1980s in widening home ownership has not been maintained.

Portable pensions, PEPs and schemes to encourage young entrepreneurs were not random ideas designed to deal on an ad hoc basis with current problems. Rather, along with the privatisation of state assets, the promotion of profit sharing schemes and the sale of council houses, they were part of a coherent pattern designed to produce a sense of independence, self-sufficiency and social belonging in the individual.

As the political philosopher Shirley Letwin noted:

> The Thatcherite argues that being one's own master – in the sense of owning one's home or disposing of one's property – provides an incentive to think differently about the world. The case can most easily be understood by contrast with the diametrical opposite, an individual who owns practically nothing in the world, rents his lodgings, has no savings or pension, depends for his earnings on a remote impersonal employer, and is, in short, wholly at the mercy of others for all the necessities of life. Such an individual would need to be a remarkable character if he were to retain a moral sense of independence and self-sufficiency ... The Thatcherite argues that an owner who feels that he is 'in charge' and 'secure' is more likely to be active, to take risks, to display initiative.

Vinson was not familiar with the writing of Dr Letwin, but it should be clear from the passages above, as well as from the preceding chapters, that he had reached very similar conclusions long before the term 'Thatcherism' had even been invented.

To Vinson's regret, the achievements of the 1980s and early '90s have been partly eroded by the failure of the Conservative Party's leadership to pursue the creation of a property-owning democracy as a central objective – and particularly failing to recognise that excessive land rationing was the major obstacle to home ownership. Over four decades, the land value of a plot – and the mortgage cost, commensurably – has more than doubled to over 50 per cent of the cost of a house, thus pricing out the lower paid.

By 1981, as a result of the Right to Buy measures, the proportion of those owning their home was greater than the number of those renting. Data extrapolated from the 2011 Census shows that home ownership reached a peak of 69 per cent in 2001, but fell back to 64 per cent in 2010. The proportion of those buying with a mortgage is also down from a high of 42 per cent in 1998 to 36 per cent in 2012, reflecting the smaller number of young people entering the property market.

Share ownership is also in decline, partly as a result of the market's mediocre performance following the dotcom bubble and the financial crisis. UK individuals now directly own 11.5 per cent of UK stocks, down from 16.7 per cent in 1998 and 54 per cent in 1963. Encouraged by the Financial Services Authority, British pension funds have also reduced their equity holdings, preferring the safer haven of corporate and government bonds instead, thus reducing people's indirect shareholdings. Foreign investors now account for 42 per cent of London-listed shares, compared with 28 per cent in 1997.

Under the present government, the proportion of those owning shares has halved, but, in the 2014 Budget, they did finally acknowledge the importance of share owner-ship, putting forward measures to improve tax breaks in respect of ISAs and allow early access to individual pension funds – a real step towards recognising that people can be trusted to manage their own financial affairs. In good time too, for, as a perceptive observer noted in April 2013:

> Fewer people feel that they own a stake in our eco-nomic system. It is no surprise, therefore, that old fashioned class war is returning: one of the most per-nicious threats to capitalism today is the widespread feeling that the wages of workers, including much of the middle classes, are falling behind while cor-porate profits keep going up.[7]

---

7 Allister Heath, 'Thatcher's property-owning democracy needs to be rescued', *Daily Telegraph*, 23 April 2013.

Press reports appearing a few days after the death of Margaret Thatcher on 8 April 2013 suggested that new measures to encourage share ownership were to be included in the 2015 Conservative Party manifesto. However, Vinson suspects the words that came from the Downing Street press office amounted to no more than a guilty admission of the government's central objective being lost by a Prime Minister without a strong political philosophy.

Among the surviving Thatcherites, Vinson understands as well as anyone the power of popular capitalism to restore national wealth and confidence – and thus arrest national decline. He is heartened to see this advocated across a broad spectrum of the press, individuals and think tanks.

CHAPTER 9

Life in the Lords

THERE ARE MANY instances of public figures seeking more prestigious honours than those offered, but few, if any, ask for a lesser award. As the date of the publication of the honours list approaches, the Downing Street staff are accustomed to receiving telephone calls from those who believe that their services to mankind merit considerably greater recognition than proposed. The compilers have, consequently, become skilled in tactfully rejecting such heartfelt entreaties. The example of Nigel Vinson is, however, an unusual one.

When informed by post that Margaret Thatcher was to recommend a baronetcy be bestowed upon him by Her Majesty in recognition of his public service, Vinson misunderstood the contents of the letter.

He explained:

> Having been unpaid chairman of the Rural Development Commission for six years I knew I was due for some sort of recognition. I had always assumed this would be a knighthood. I had rather liked this idea. But I am not terribly well informed about the workings of the honours system and I stupidly didn't understand the letter. Consequently, when I returned home that evening I told my wife, 'I am now Sir Nigel and you are now Lady Vinson.' But when I showed her the letter, she told me that I was being offered a peerage, which at the time wasn't what I wanted at all.

Vinson – soon to be Baron Vinson of Roddam Dene – telephoned Ian Gow, Mrs Thatcher's PPS and a good personal friend, to explain that he would far prefer to be knighted than to be elevated to the peerage. But Gow, for whom

Vinson had huge respect and admiration, was emphatic that he was wanted in the Lords.

> I suppose subconsciously I may have been influenced by the fact that, as a child, my mother read to me *Sir Nigel* by Arthur Conan Doyle. My boyhood impression was that knights were heroes on white horses who went around rescuing maidens from distress, while barons were wicked people who ground the faces of the poor.
>
> More seriously, when I realised what was being proposed I was worried that it might impact on our relations with our neighbours in my adopted county of Northumberland. It's not that becoming a peer changes you, but you fear that other people's perception of you will change, that a barrier will come down that didn't previously exist. They expect you to be different, even if you carry on behaving in exactly the same way.
>
> In the event that hasn't happened and I am not sorry that I accepted. When you are arguing your corner or fighting for something you believe in people do take more notice of you if you happen to be a lord. Sadly, such influence has diminished over time.

Vonnie had been emphatic that he should accept the peerage.

Nigel was extremely reluctant, but I knew that it would give him an opportunity to express his views and to gain support for causes he believed in. It was just right for him. The title did not change my life in any way, but it provided Nigel with a new means to pursue longstanding aims.

Vinson believes that the respect in which peers were formerly held has been undermined by Tony Blair's mass appointments to the upper chamber, the general decline in public regard for Parliament, and the introduction of a system of peers' expenses that has opened up the possibility of malfeasance. Nigel reports that the quality of food in the Lords' dining room has risen, while the standard of manners has gone down; the quality of debate remains high, though it goes mostly unreported; sadly, the chamber's ability to rectify problems and serve the national good has declined: 'A generation ago, peers were respected, had prestige and the power and influence that comes with it. When going abroad we were asked to inform the appropriate embassy – be updated on policy and offered help if needed. We were regarded as being in a quasi-ambassadorial role.'

It would seem that even the legitimate fringe benefits of being a peer have also diminished.

Shortly after being elevated to the Upper House, Nigel realised that business in the chamber was running late and that he and several other peers would miss their train home. Having got the number from a House of Lords researcher, Nigel rang the station master at King's Cross and said to him: 'Station master, six of your regular peers are going to miss the seven o'clock to Edinburgh this evening due to an over-run of business. Could you possibly hold up the train for a few minutes – or we won't get home?'

When Nigel and his colleagues arrived at ten past seven, they found the station master and, more importantly, the train waiting for them. 'We have plenty of catch-up time on this journey and I am pleased to have helped you, sir,' the station master said. Nigel doubts whether members of the House of Lords would be treated with the same respect today; he believes that we are in 'the twilight of authority'.

A minor matter illustrates this point. The renowned seared liver is no longer served in the House of Lords – banned as dangerous by the Westminster Health Officer – and, when told, Vinson exploded: 'Their Lordships are even told what they mustn't eat! *Sic transit Gloria.*'

In his maiden speech in 1984, Nigel referred to the fact that a number of peers had asked him the reason why he had chosen Baron Vinson of Roddam Dene as his title.

He explained:

> It happens to be where I live, and it is also an area of
> special scientific interest because it contains a unique
> geological formation. The formation has many similar
> properties to a bad speech. You could say, my lords,
> that it has gone on a long time and that it is dull, thick
> and not very exciting. It will be a constant reminder
> for me to keep my speeches short.

Nigel Vinson continues to sit on the Conservative benches,
and has proved to be a conscientious, well-informed and
independent-minded member. According to Matt Ridley,
who sits alongside him in the Lords, Vinson's independence
of mind is both admired and respected by his parliamen-
tary colleagues.

Vinson has also established a reputation for his deep
and sympathetic understanding of the problems of business – 'a trading nation simply cannot ignore the rate of
exchange at which it trades' – as well as those of the rural
economy. He also proved to be a perceptive early critic of
fashionable environmental panaceas, and a robust, knowledgeable opponent of British EU membership. This is
an issue that presently occupies him to a greater extent
than any other.

Although Vinson is now an opponent of the EU, this has not always been the case. In common with many other Thatcherites, including Keith Joseph, Nicholas Ridley and Margaret Thatcher herself, he voted to stay in Europe in the 1975 referendum. He did so in the belief that what was being constructed was largely a commercial undertaking, whereby membership would enable Britain to sell its goods more easily to an expanding European market. He saw it as a continuation of our historic trade relationship with Europe – as exemplified by the woolsack in the House of Lords.

Vinson's first doubts about the wisdom of having joined the European project came about as a result of his farming activities. Although the recipient of EU farm subsidies, he became gradually aware of the colossal waste and inefficiency EU regulations produced, and the impossibility of doing anything to remedy this situation.

> Whenever I railed against an EU regulation on the grounds that the danger or hazard that it was intended to deal with didn't exist and that there was no evidence to suggest that it did, the regulation was justified by reference to the precautionary principle. On that basis it is possible to justify almost *any* regulation.

His Euroscepticism grew as a result of the scare over Creutzfeldt–Jakob disease (CJD), a matter symptomatic of a wider EU malaise. The UK has by far the biggest sheep industry in Europe, yet it is totally regulated from Brussels. In 2002, the EU introduced measures requiring farmers to split the carcasses of sheep older than twelve months in order to remove the spinal cord – an expensive process that can add £5 to the cost of a sheep. The controls also had the effect of taking mutton off the market since farmers have an incentive to sell before the sheep is one year old. In France, the regulations are enforced through a system of vacuum spinal cord removal – a process costing half as much as the British method.

To date, no scientific evidence of any kind has been produced to show that the sources of CJD, a degenerative and fatal neurological disorder, can be traced to lamb. Indeed, the National Farmers Union has actually pointed to scientific evidence discounting this possibility – but the regulations remain in place. Meanwhile, Britain continues to import French sheep carcasses and sheep from other EU countries where the regulation does not apply because the flock size is less than 4,000 and, as a result, falls outside the scope of the legislation.

In April 2011, Vinson wrote to Lord Rooker, chairman of the Food Standards Agency, to try to get the regulation lifted:

If our industry were to adopt the French method of
vacuum spinal cord removal it would at least go half
way to reducing the cost. It is ludicrous that we can
import French carcases… However, it is total abolition
of this outdated regulation that is required. Is this not
a goal the FSA could set itself to help make our poor
battered economy more efficient?

While noting Lord Vinson's comments about the need
for regulatory change, Rooker replied: 'The aim is to continue a process of step-by-step change, based on scientific
evidence, while maintaining a high level of consumer
protection.'

Four years on, the reality is that the consumer remains
'protected' against a non-existent threat – to the detriment
of UK farmers and British shoppers – through a system that
is needlessly expensive. This is only one of the many similar
challenges to bad regulation Vinson has made over time.

As Vinson also points out, still more expensive is the
European Drinking Water Directive, which imposed standards of water purity that, in Nigel's view, clearly exceeded
those necessary to ensure public health. The enforcement,
estimated to have cost the UK billions of pounds, is another
example of the misplaced application of the precautionary principle.

In a speech to the House of Lords in 2009, Vinson pointed out that the net cost of UK membership to the EU was £12 billion per annum, although the total cost was higher since it could not be assumed the rebates were being spent on sensible purposes approved by the UK Treasury. However, this figure paled into insignificance when measured against the cost of unnecessary regulations – which, Nigel suggested, almost certainly ran into the tens of billions. He named four he regarded as particularly damaging to Britain's economic well-being: the working time directive; the chemicals directive; the height at work directive; and the pesticides directive.

He told his fellow peers:

> All these things, like the premature closing down of our coal power stations just when we need them, chisel away and do real economic damage to our flexible economy. It is not as if we could do anything about it, anything to rectify it in any way. Here Parliament, through its scrutiny committee, has tried to influence that legislation, but its work has been almost totally ignored. Hundreds of recommendations have been made to improve EU legislation and the hard fact is that our scrutiny committees have been wasting their time. Frustratingly, there is no satisfactory way

of rectifying that regulation. The democratic safety valve does not exist...

Our blind and damaging conformity to EU regulations is like an army marching over a cliff because no one has the courage to question the command. Few in Westminster realise what is going on; the political class lives above it all ... I love my country and I hate to see it ruined by bureaucratic nonsenses imposed by non-elected, totally impractical officials.

Partly as a consequence of his experience as a hill farmer, Vinson was an early critic of 'gold plating', whereby EU regulations and directives are translated into British law in a more extreme form than in most other EU countries. Unlike other Eurosceptics, however, he did not wholly blame this on the zealotry of British officials, understanding correctly that this phenomenon was the consequence of the fundamental differences between Britain and continental Europe in terms of legal philosophy and traditions:

In this country, under common law, everything is legal except that which is declared to be illegal. In Europe, under Roman law, everything is illegal except that which is specifically allowed, although interpretations of the law are conditioned by the principles of proportionality and *de minimis*. This made it almost inevitable that when EU law was transformed into British law the latter would be more stringent than in continental law because of the mandatory character of the former. It is no use just blaming officials: the problem is deeply rooted in our history and political culture.

In a memorable speech in a House of Lords debate in 2004 Lord Vinson pointed out that in the preceding years there had been 27,000 items of legislation, covering 97,000 pages of instruction. He observed: 'It is never wrong to be reminded that Dean Swift, in his allegory *Gulliver's Travels*, was attempting to tackle the same problem. He said of Gulliver: "No one silken thread held him down, but a thousand made him immobile." We need to start cutting those threads.'

The total regulatory costs were immense – estimated by the British Chamber of Commerce to amount to £20 billion over the previous five years. However, the problem was not just one of making more appropriate regulation but also of unscrambling existing regulation where it had become inappropriate or no longer necessary. In particular, it was extremely difficult to unscramble safety legislation because those who tried to do so could so easily be accused of not caring whether somebody was killed or injured. As Nigel said:

In our safety-ridden society we are advised that decisions are best based on the precautionary principle. In effect, that enables any authority to abandon the concept of risk assessment and balanced judgment based on proportionality. Precaution is so much easier to justify than proportion. The avoidance of risk does not have to be justified, because who can be brave enough to challenge publicly the concept of putting safety above all else? Thus the precautionary principle stifles rational scientific debate regarding the nature of risk and is often nothing more than the cloak for intellectual cowardice.

Opponents of excessive regulation have delighted in pointing to striking examples of absurd or unnecessary legislation – from regulations governing the shape of cucumbers to those requiring horses to be issued with passports – but Vinson came up with a brave and original example of his own – aircraft safety jackets.

He told his fellow peers:

> I have checked and found that not once in the past twenty-five years had lifejackets been fitted prior to an accident on a passenger aircraft. Even if they had been, I doubt whether they would have had much

practical good, because a jumbo jet hitting the water
at any speed would disintegrate and sink rapidly. There
is an inherent risk in aircraft – thank God they have a
fantastic safety record. The demonstration fitting of
lifejackets does nothing, except perhaps to comfort
passengers – or to cause them concern. Nobody has
yet had the courage to suggest that this useless safety
charade should be discontinued.

Vinson went on to lambast lawyers for exploiting the obses-
sion with safety:

We live in an increasingly safety-conscious age, a liti-
gious age. Sadly, many lawyers who used to run their
practices with an ethos of what is good for society – *pro
bono publico* – now do so wholly to exploit the system
under the maxim, 'Where there's blame, there's a
claim.' An increasing number of lawyers, like leeches,
bleed the rest of us white. I often wonder, too, whether
some of our judiciary understand that it is not just an
insurance company that pays, but ultimately their fellow citizens. Many people feel that somehow society
must reverse this ethos of blame.

However, the problem is wider than that. It is damaging the whole concept of personal self-reliance. If

we are encouraged to believe that it is never our fault and always somebody else's, that we are not responsible for our own actions, that it is the fault of the society in which we live and not we ourselves, that it is the seller's fault and not ours, we undermine the whole basis of our historic laws. If we substitute *caveat vendor* – let the seller beware – for *caveat emptor* – let the buyer beware – we reverse the whole concept of blame by denying responsibility for our own actions.

He concluded: 'Apart from the economic consequences of excessive regulation, the greatest unintended consequence is that the denial of personal responsibility becomes embedded in our culture. The road to national decline is paved with well-intentioned regulations.'

By the time the Maastricht Treaty was signed in 1992, Vinson – who had cut short a family holiday in Venice to return home alone in order to vote against the ratification of the treaty – had come to the conclusion that the costs of British membership greatly outweighed the benefits. In his view, these benefits were either grossly exaggerated or simply illusory.

By that time I had concluded that the ideas which animated the European project, together with the self-serving interests of the commission, made the EU unreformable; it was clear that any attempt to make it more democratic would be subverted and end up having the opposite effect. This is precisely what happened with Giscard's Convention on the Future of Europe, whose explicit purpose was to solve the problem of the 'democratic deficit' by bringing ordinary people and the political elites closer together – but which instead ended up producing a constitution for a centralised European state.

Subsequent events and the attempt to exploit every crisis, financial or otherwise, which has befallen the EU in order to achieve its ever closer political and economic integration, have confirmed my view. Most of all I have been angered by the fact that none of us has any power to change things which are so obviously wrong. The European Scrutiny Committee has failed utterly in reversing bad legislation. The American War of Independence was fought on the slogan 'No taxation without representation.' We now have the modern equivalent: 'Regulation without rectification.' If one cannot change regulations through elected representatives then democracy is in denial. If you cannot sack those who rule you, you no longer have sovereignty.

If, like his fellow parliamentarians, he could do nothing about getting rid of the regulations that did more harm than good, or which had outlived their usefulness, he concluded that he could at least do something to help small business individuals who found themselves unfairly accused of breaching regulations by overzealous officials, especially ones relating to health and safety. The result was the 1994 Deregulation and Contracting Out Bill, for which he obtained party backing and saw passed into law later that year. For the first time, those who were wrongly accused of breaking the rules were given legal redress.

Vinson believes that, although the legislation was subsequently weakened by Labour amendments, the impact was a cultural shift that resulted in a more balanced and common sense approach to the interpretation of the rules – a belief borne out by the gradual disappearance from our newspaper columns of grotesque examples of rules being applied in a disproportionate or absurd way.

In the main, Vinson preferred his work in the Lords' economic committee to participating in big set-piece debates, but not all of his thoughts centred on micro-economic policy, Europe or the consequences of unnecessary or badly designed regulation.

In 2004, Nigel introduced a bill to improve the lives of the villagers in the tiny hamlet of Holburn near his home.

When selling his farms at Hetton, he had decided he would like to record his association with the area and its people by donating a parcel of land that would become the village green. To his surprise, he found the legal process involved in transferring and registering land to common owner-ship so complex and difficult that it was almost impossible.

After lengthy discussions with the parish council, North-umberland council, DEFRA and his lawyers, Nigel resolved the problem by donating the land, which included an early nineteenth-century fountain, to the parish coun-cil. In accordance with their benefactor's wishes, the council then dedicated it as a village green. However, in order to make it easier for landowners to transfer parcels of prop-erty into common ownership – and perhaps to encourage more of them to do so – Vinson introduced the Commons Bill in November 2004. This shortened and simplified the legal processes of donating land for such purposes.

A simple and unpretentious plaque erected on the site of Holburn Village Green reads: 'Given by the Vinson fam-ily who farmed the Hettons 1971–2002.'

Today, the green is used by the villagers as well as those from neighbouring hamlets during the annual village fair and other special occasions.

Outside the Lords, Vinson threw his weight behind oth-ers campaigning for the UK's withdrawal from the EU, irrespective of party allegiance. In a foreword to a publication urging British withdrawal he wrote: 'Like other countries, we could manage perfectly well outside Europe: we are a global trading nation. Britain must discover that democracy means self-governance and that self-governance only works with national independence. In every respect we would be better off out.'

The pro-EU views of Graham Mather, who had taken over the general directorship of the IEA from Ralph Harris, was one of the factors that led Vinson, as its chairman, to side with the founders in an acrimonious public row, which led to Mather's departure in 1992. For supporting them over this difficult time, Ralph and Arthur honoured Vinson by making him life trustee of the IEA. Mather subsequently became an MEP and President of the European Policy Forum, while his job at the IEA was filled on a temporary basis, but with distinction, by Russell Lewis, a Eurosceptic-minded former leader writer for the *Daily Telegraph* and *Daily Mail.* Under Vinson's chairmanship they continued to have high-level meetings with international economists, the governor of the Bank of England and the Treasury, where Vinson would advance his belief that corporation tax should be abolished and companies should be obliged to distribute more of their profits by way of taxable dividends. After Lewis, the post was taken up by John Blundell, a longstanding opponent of British membership of the EU.

For three years, from 2008 to 2011, Vinson served as chairman of the Better Off Out Group, one of the organisations that kept Euroscepticism alive at a time when Britain's political elites, and in particular the BBC, depicted those wishing to take Britain out of the EU as extreme, unbalanced and possibly racist. Ian Milne – a longstanding, scholarly advocate of UK withdrawal, the founder of the Eurosceptic publication *Eurofacts* and the creator of the think tank Global Britain – was among the individual writers and campaigners given support and encouragement in their struggle to bring about a new relationship with Europe.

'My two books on the EU might not have seen the light of day without Nigel's help,' Milne told me:

> I was given personal funding for the first, which was entitled *A Cost too Far* and attempted a cost-benefit analysis of membership. He was also instrumental in getting the think tank Civitas, of which he is a trustee, to publish it.
>
> In the case of the second, *Time to Say No*, which deals with the alternatives to EU membership, I planned to self-publish and approached Nigel to ask whether he would help meet the printer's bill. He correctly

pointed out that I lacked the means to achieve a wide distribution and he again persuaded Civitas to publish. It has since gone into a second edition.

In August 2012, Vinson, a former chairman of his constituency party and president of the Berwick-upon-Tweed Conservative Association, made no secret of the fact that he would prefer to see the Conservative Party led by Boris Johnson. He also told his local newspaper the *Newcastle Journal* that he and other peers would switch their support to UKIP unless David Cameron adopted a more robust policy on EU membership:

> Like many Tories, I will consider going to UKIP unless Cameron does something serious about repatriating powers. I and many others will leave the Conservative Party unless we get a clear signal from Cameron because our relationship with Europe is extremely damaging and we would be better off out.

Vinson had no desire to cause long-term damage to the political party to which he had belonged for nearly all his adult life, but he passionately wished to halt the continuing erosion of national sovereignty. Cameron's introduction of the Referendum Bill in the autumn of 2013, in response to the rise of UKIP, has, to date, prevented Nigel from carrying out his threat.

Vinson believes that one of his finest speeches was delivered during a debate on the Climate Change Bill in November 2007, during which he criticised the bill for being too complex and over-regulatory, correctly forecasting that the limits it sought to impose on CO_2 emissions would be unachievable. The speech also pointed out that, in a global context, the contribution Britain could make would not even be scientifically measurable – the underlying problem was too many people; a population exploding on a limited planet.

He said that carbon trading, which the bill sought to promote, had been rightly described as a scam, and continued:

> Carbon trading is a charter for international cheating through bogus assessments and fraudulent verification. I doubt whether in practice it achieves anything worthwhile.
>
> Trading our carbon inputs with the undeveloped world is the modern equivalent of selling one's sins to gain redemption. If such trading accelerates the introduction of sensible measures that really will reduce carbon on a massive scale, so much the better, but I am doubtful. The whole concept is full of holes.

Vinson also deplored the tendency to treat energy use as if it were somehow unworthy:

> Energy use is the foundation of civilisation – ours in particular. Economic self-flagellation through enforced target setting would be deeply damaging to the economy and an expensive way of setting an example. In any case, it will be totally ignored by India, South America and China, whose energy footprint is due to overtake that of the US very shortly.

The solution he proposed was a greater reliance on electricity generated by nuclear power. 'There is hope for the globe, but not through micromanagement, over-regulatory measures and the unrealistic thinking that this bill promotes', he concluded.

Despite his advancing years, Vinson continues to bombard the government at question time and through his submission of written questions on a wide range of subjects, knowing that replies have to be signed off by the minister or head of department. This therefore provides him an opportunity to make government officials aware of matters that might otherwise fail to engage their attention. The full list of his concerns, most of them described elsewhere in this book, is lengthy; but, latterly, most have centred on the anti-democratic nature of the European project, the high cost of Britain's net EU budget contribution, the EU Arrest Warrant, and Britain's huge ongoing trade deficit. In his speech on the European Referendum Bill – which he doubts will ever achieve the repatriation of powers he believes this country needs – Vinson concluded:

> Frankly, I believe it is impossible to be a democrat today and to support our continued membership of an unreformed European Union. It is time this matter was put to the British people – we want our country back; we do not want to be a region in the republic of Europe.

Although he regrets the declining influence of the upper chamber, he does not regret having entered it: 'It has given me a chance to try to correct wrongs as I see them, and for that I am profoundly grateful.'

Postscript

O N THE OCCASION of his seventieth birth-day, Nigel decided to publish an anthology of favourite quotations, sayings, poems and literary texts, which he had collected over the years and kept in a scrap box. This also included extracts from his own speeches and occasional writings. He entitled the resulting volume *Take Upon Retiring* – to indicate that the best time to read such a book might be at bedtime or, indeed, when fully retired. To give the book a distinctive appearance, he chose a square format, wide margins and a variety of fonts and type sizes. Intended as a way of passing onto his daughters and grandchildren an account of what he thought about the world, the lessons he had learned in life and the things he had picked up from others, 750 copies of this elegantly produced volume were printed by a Berwick-upon-Tweed family firm, and copies were sent to his friends.

To his evident pleasure, Nigel received a stream of requests for copies from people who had heard about the book, or seen it when visiting mutual friends, along with a number of suggestions about items that might have been included. As a result, he published an expanded and updated version on his seventy-fifth birthday – entitled *Take Upon Retiring – Late Extra*.

In the book, he prescribed a pattern for living:

> *First twenty years learning,*
> *Second twenty years earning,*
> *Third twenty years putting in,*
> *Fourth twenty years taking out – well, partly.*

Vinson has not entirely followed this prescription, at least not in the fourth quarter of his life. Brought up to recognise that the privileged have a responsibility to society, he is still putting in. However, he maintains he did more good for the world through the huge advances in productivity he developed at Plastic Coatings – 'creating wealth out of things rather than making money out of money' – than through anything he did subsequently.

Now in his eighty-fifth year, Vinson continues to speak in the Lords and take an active part in the workings of the Upper House. He is quick on his feet to make salient points at question time and keeps up his barrage of written enquiries – even if he has cut down the number of visits to London.

Nigel's speech on the family problems he thought would follow the bill legalising same-sex marriage in July 2013 was one of the most forceful and passionately argued in a debate that clearly exceeded the quality of its relative in the Commons. This debating prowess was continued later that year, when he strongly argued in favour of 'assisted dying'.

Although his business activities have been cut back, the land he farms comprises only a fraction of the 4,000 acres he once owned. He no longer hunts, but he does continue to ride on a daily basis, despite occasional falls.

However, while he has divested himself of most of his company directorships, he takes sole responsibility for investing the assets of the Nigel Vinson Charitable Trust, which he founded more than forty years ago with an initial contribution of £100,000. Into this he has poured two-thirds of the proceeds from the sale of the Roddam Estate, thus enabling him to greatly expand the scope of his charitable giving.

Over the last decade, the trust has outperformed the FTSE 100 by an impressive margin, its aim being: 'to promote the understanding of the constitution of liberty through support, education and research of those bodies that advance its importance to a free society.'

His continued interest in the activities of the charities, think tanks and pressure groups he has supported over the decades reflects an undiminished interest in public affairs. The IEA, Civitas, the CPS, the Freedom Association, the TaxPayers' Alliance, Reform and Politeia all continue to benefit from his support, and new causes and projects also have been added to the list (not least Nigel's plotting with Professor Ian Fells over what could be done to enable this country to develop small modular factory-built reactors – 'the energy source of the future', as they saw it).

Moreover, no visitor to his home is likely to leave without hearing several suggestions about how current economic or political problems might be solved.

The sale of Roddam Hall reflected a desire to leave his affairs in good order – 'we wanted to halve the job for our executors' – so his family would not be burdened with legal complexities on his death.

It is typical of his practical and considerate nature that,

when we agreed I would write this biography, he left instruction that, should he die before completion, his executors would extend every cooperation. This, however, was followed up by another request: I should organise my research and writing in such a way that, if *I* were to die first, another author could take over!

Success in business, trusting people irrespective of position, a clear grasp of his life ambitions, remarkably good health, a discerning eye and sound judgement have all meant that Nigel has been able to organise and fulfil most of his interests – business, farming, horses, *objets d'art*, buildings, good food and enjoyment of the countryside – while quietly attempting to make a better world. Quick-witted and inventive by nature, he has the ability to provoke the laughter – or groans – of others, without malice. Cruel remarks or jibes produce obvious signs of distaste from him. His cheerfulness is indestructible, but he would prefer to talk about serious matters rather than human weakness – 'more bread than circuses', as he puts it. This sets him apart from many of those who occupy the Westminster village.

The year 2014 saw two developments in which Vinson could take justifiable pride.

First, the government announced a set of measures to enable small companies to retain their profits untaxed (if reinvested), enjoy greater access to finance and reduce the burden of red tape – something Nigel had first advocated almost half a century before.

Second, a renascent CPS, the think tank Vinson had personally helped Keith Joseph and Margaret Thatcher found, celebrated its fortieth anniversary with a conference at the Guildhall. Addressing guests at a dinner for speakers and invited VIPs from around the world, including the Chancellor of the Exchequer George Osborne, Nigel Vinson reminded everyone of the principles the centre had been established to promote:

> They [the CPS founders] sought policies that worked with the grain of human nature. It was becoming obvious to them that when the state owns nobody owns and when nobody owns nobody cares. Hence their underlying belief in the alternative – a property-owning democracy and a free-market economy where wealth and power are well diffused – above all they recognised that compassion without resource is ineffective, and thus the key to compassion is the creation of wealth. This indeed is at the heart of the moral case for capitalism. But capitalism is not perfect, and needs a strong moral, legal and democratic framework to operate successfully and fairly, and one which enables errors to be exposed to enable correction.

Vinson's speech received a warm and emotional response from those present, and encapsulated an approach to life and politics to which he has remained true in both actions and words.

Now enjoying his part-retirement – still addicted to chocolate, riding with his neighbour Sir Humphry Wakefield, and making bows and arrows culled from traditional churchyard yews for his grandchildren – he remains active to the last.

This short and affectionate biography – written by a friend who wishes to record his thanks for the support he has received over many years – is the story of a man not widely known outside his adopted county of Northumberland, but who has played an important, if largely unrecognised, role in the public life of his country. Its title – *Making Things Happen* – was chosen because of its subject's long record of organising resources, whether economic or intellectual, to solve problems.

As Margaret Thatcher recognised, without Vinson, the CPS might never have been established; without Vinson, it might have taken many more years to bring flexibility and common sense to the structure and organisation of Britain's pensions industry; without Vinson, the plans to encourage private saving might well have taken longer to coalesce.

Without Nigel's committed direction, the Queen's

Silver Jubilee Appeal might well have raised less money – and, subsequently, the Prince's Trust might be less well endowed. Without Nigel's leadership of the RDC, it would have taken considerably longer to breathe new life into Britain's rural economy. Without Nigel's backing, a great number of reformers – mostly of Conservative or classical liberal persuasion – would have found it harder to achieve their goals. Some might have failed completely.

If today's workplace is, in some respects, more human and less prone to disputes on class or ideological grounds, it is because of the developments Nigel Vinson encouraged through example and persuasion. Numerous organisations to which he has given his time have undoubtedly been bettered by his counsel and masterclass in common sense. There are, consequently, many people who have benefitted from Nigel's ability to think originally, get to the heart of a matter and do something to help – most of these people are not even aware of his input.

An unusual combination of determination, cheerfulness and inventiveness has underpinned Nigel Vinson's support for friends in need and the local community in the remote part of Northumberland in which he has chosen to live. These same qualities have been apparent in his lifelong search for answers to complex economic and political problems.

As his eldest daughter Bettina commented: 'He is a man who is incapable of passing by on the other side.'

Timeline of Lord Vinson
of Roddam Dene
LVO DL FRSA FBIM

1931

27 January: NV born at Nettlestead Place, Kent; second son of Ronald and Bettina (née Southwell-Sander) Vinson

1939

NV enters Brambletye Preparatory School, East Grinstead

1944

NV enters Pangbourne Naval College, Berkshire

1947–8

NV becomes cadet captain at Pangbourne Naval College

1948

NV travels to South Africa, visiting what was then Rhodesia and Mozambique in a second-hand car; spends eighteenth birthday in Kruger National Park

1949–51

NV undertakes national service in the army; serves as Lieutenant in Queens Royal Regiment at 3 Brigade in Egypt and Weapons Training Officer at Shorncliffe

1951

NV starts work on the bench at Creators Ltd of Woking

1952

Durable Plastics is registered as a limited company and begins operations from a Nissen hut in Friary Square, Guildford

1956

Durable Plastics moves to purpose-built factory in Woodbridge Meadows, Guildford

NV becomes chairman of Guildford Young Conservatives

1958

NV becomes chairman of Guildford Young Enterprise

1960

Durable Plastics changes its name to Plastic Coatings

1961

NV becomes director of *Kentish Times* (until 1966)

1964

Working Together Campaign publishes NV's pamphlet 'Towards a common purpose in industry – involvement in the smaller unit'

1967

NV joins the CBI Council

NV sits on the board of the Trade Investment Grants Committee (until 1971)

NV becomes governor of Brambletye School (until 1971)

NV delivers lecture to the IPA entitled 'How we tackled the problem of involvement'

1968

NV joins CBI taxation committee

NV becomes director of the Sugar Board (until 1975)

1969

Plastic Coatings floats by tender on the London Stock Exchange

1971

NV receives the Queen's Award for industry recognising PCL's technological innovation

PCL receives the Design Council Award

NV becomes chairman and managing director of PCL (until 1972)

NV becomes chairman of the Industrial Participation Association (until 1978; then president 1979–90)

NV becomes member of the NHS Pharmaceutical Services Committee

NV becomes member of the Institute of Directors Council

NV becomes member of the Crafts Advisory Committee (until 1977)

Imperial Group buys controlling interest in PCL

NV buys Roddam Estate, Northumberland

1972

NV stands down as CEO of PCL to become non-executive chairman

NV joins the CBI president's committee

NV becomes chairman of the Crafts Council of Great Britain which, under his leadership, becomes the Crafts Advisory Council, subsequently the Crafts Council

NV becomes trustee of the IEA (until 2004; life vice president thereafter)

NV becomes director of the Fleming High Income Growth Trust (chairman 1995–2001)

NV is founder donor of Martin Mere Wildfowl Reserve

NV buys Hetton Estate, Northumberland

NV marries Yvonne Ann Collin

1973

NV becomes director of British Airports Authority (until 1980)

NV becomes member of the Design Council (until 1980)

NV becomes director of David Nieper Ltd (until 1979)

NV is made a Fellow of the Royal Society of Arts

NV is made a Fellow of the British Institute of Management

NV restores Roddam Hall

NV buys Vinosmena estate in Spain

1974

NV is the founding director and honorary treasurer of the CPS (standing down in 1980)

NV becomes chairman of the Wider Ownership Group

NV becomes member of the King George VI Jubilee Trust Council (until 1978)

23 July: Bettina Vinson born at Chelsea and Westminster Hospital, London

1975

NV becomes director of the Electra Investment Trust (until 1998; deputy chairman 1990–98)

NV moves to restored Roddam Hall

NV becomes a trustee of the Farne Islands (until 1985)

NV becomes director of Barclays Bank in the north east region (until 1979)

NV becomes honorary director of the Queen's Silver Jubilee Appeal (until 1978)

1977

NV becomes member of the Northumberland National Parks Countryside Committee (until 1989)

NV becomes member of the Regional Committee National Trust (until 1984)

19 April: Rowena Vinson born at Pembury Hospital, Kent

1979

NV invested as Lieutenant of the Royal Victorian Order in recognition of his personal services to the Queen

NV becomes deputy chairman of the CBI's Smaller Firms Council (until 1984)

NV becomes president of the Industrial Participation Association (until 1989; chairman 1971–78)

NV speaks at a seminar at the IEA on the role of the entrepreneur; contribution is subsequently published in *Prime Movers of Progress*

11 April: Antonia Vinson born at Roddam Hall

4 May: Conservatives win general election; Margaret Thatcher becomes Britain's first woman Prime Minister

1980

NV made chairman of the RDC (until 1990) by Margaret Thatcher

NV becomes chairman of the Council of Small Industries in Rural Areas (until 1982)

NV becomes church warden of Ilderton Church, Northumberland

1982

NV becomes director of Barclays Bank UK (until 1988)

1983

NV becomes chairman of the National Trust Cragside Appeal

1984

NV publishes 'Personal and Portable Pensions – For All'

NV publishes 'Owners All'

1985

NV made a life peer in recognition of his public service; becomes Lord Vinson of Roddam Dene

NV becomes chairman of the Industry Year Steering Committee RSA (until 1987)

NV becomes chairman of the Newcastle Technology Centre (until 1988)

22 July: NV appears on BBC's *Any Questions*

1986

NV becomes chairman of the Bamburgh Castle Trustees

1989

NV becomes chairman of trustees at the IEA (until 1995)

NV becomes chairman of St Cuthbert's Newcastle Estates (until 2000)

NV sells his estate in Spain

1990

NV becomes member of the Council of St George's House, Windsor Castle (until 1996)

NV made Deputy Lieutenant of Northumberland

NV becomes deputy chairman of the Electra Investment Trust

1992

NV becomes director of Mercury World Mining

4 June: NV delivers the Annual Enterprise Lecture at Durham Business School entitled 'Charity Begins at Work'

1994

NV becomes chairman of Fuel Tech, USA (until 1996)

NV delivers a Fabian Society lecture on pensions

1997

NV becomes chairman of Prince's Trust in the north east region (until 2000)

1998

NV becomes life vice-president of the IEA

1999

NV becomes chairman of the North East Civic Trust (until 2001)

2000

NV publishes *Take Upon Retiring*

2001

NV becomes member of the House of Lords select committee on economic affairs (until 2003)

NV becomes member of the Council of Freedom Association

NV sells Hetton Estate

2003

NV becomes chairman of the Berwick-upon-Tweed
Conservative Association (until 2005)

2004

NV becomes a trustee of Civitas

NV becomes president of the Northumberland Young Farmers
Club (until 2009)

NV gifts a village green to Holburn, Northumberland

2005

NV becomes president of the Berwick-upon-Tweed
Conservative Association

NV becomes director of Grimersta Fishing

NV publishes *Take Upon Retiring – Late Extra*

2008

NV becomes chairman of the House of Lords & House of
Commons 'Better Off Out' Group (until 2011)

2009

NV becomes a trustee of the Chillingham Wild Cattle
Association

2010

NV designs and builds Roddam Rigg Farmhouse

NV sells Roddam Estate

2012

NV underwrites SongBird Survival

2013

NV becomes the patron of the Freedom Association